W

PRAISE FOR THE PREVIOUS EDITION OF
DAMNED LIES AND STATISTICS:

"Definitely a must for politicians, activists, and others who generate or use statistics, but especially for those who want to think for themselves rather than take as gospel every statistic presented to them."   —*New Scientist*

"There's a 73 percent chance that the University of Delaware prof has got our number."   —*San Diego Union-Tribune*

"Best is our leading authority on social problems today. His detective work in exposing the spurious use of statistics is essential to constructive social science. No one who speaks for the public welfare can ignore his powerful work."

—Jonathan B. Imber, Editor-in-Chief, *Society*

"Joel Best is at it again. In *Damned Lies and Statistics,* he shows how statistics are manipulated, mismanaged, misrepresented, and massaged by officials and other powerful groups to promote their agendas. He is a master at examining taken-for-granted "facts" and debunking them through careful sociological scrutiny."

—Patricia Adler, author of *Peer Power*

"In our era, numbers are as much a staple of political debates as stories. And just as stories so often turn into fables, so Best shows that we often believe the most implausible of numbers—to the detriment of us all."

Peter Reuter, coauthor of *Drug War Heresies:*
Learning from Other Vices, Times and Places

"Whether we like them or not, we have to live with statistics, and *Damned Lies and Statistics* offers a useful guide for engaging with their troublesome world. Despite the temptation to be cynical, the author of this timely and excellent work cautions the reader against reacting in such a way to statistics. What we are offered is an approach that helps us to work out the real story behind those numbers."   —*The Independent*

"*Damned Lies and Statistics* is highly entertaining as well as instructive. Best's book shows how some of those big numbers indicating big social problems were created in the first place and instructs the reader (and reporter) how to be on guard against such gross manipulation. And it doesn't take an understanding of advanced mathematics to do so thanks to this book, which ought to be required reading in every newsroom in the country."

—*Washington Times*

"The narrative flows easily, and all the points are driven home with engaging examples from real life. I found Best's book a delight. Always engaging, it is accessible to a lay reader, yet will reward the expert; the examples it gives could enrich both a primary schoolroom and a university lecture hall."   —*Nature*

"[An] absolutely fascinating and sobering quest into the fantastic differences between the world as it is and the world as it is portrayed in the statistics the media use. This book is simply a must."   —Nachman Ben-Yehuda, author of *The Masada Myth*

DAMNED LIES AND STATISTICS

DAMNED LIES

AND STATISTICS

Untangling Numbers from the

Media, Politicians, and Activists

UPDATED EDITION

Joel Best

UNIVERSITY OF CALIFORNIA PRESS

Berkeley   Los Angeles   London

University of California Press, one of the most distinguished
university presses in the United States, enriches lives around the
world by advancing scholarship in the humanities, social sciences,
and natural sciences. Its activities are supported by the UC Press
Foundation and by philanthropic contributions from individuals
and institutions. For more information, visit www.ucpress.edu.

University of California Press
Berkeley and Los Angeles, California

University of California Press, Ltd.
London, England

ISBN 978-0-520-27470-9

LIBRARY OF CONGRESS
CATALOGING-IN-PUBLICATION DATA

Best, Joel.
    Damned lies and statistics : untangling numbers from the
media, politicians, and activists / Joel Best.
        p.   cm.
    Includes bibliographical references and index.
    ISBN 978-0-520-21978-6 (cloth : alk. paper)
    1. Sociology—Statistical methods. 2. Social problems—
Statistical methods. 3. Social indicators. I. Title.
    HM535.B47   2001
    303.3'8—dc21   00-064910

Printed in the United States of America
18   17
10   9   8   7   6   5

For Kathe Lowney

CONTENTS

ACKNOWLEDGMENTS

Philip Jenkins and I originally planned to write this book together. Although Philip had too many other projects to find the time to work on this one as well, he generously suggested several examples, pointed me toward sources, and commented on drafts. I also benefited from valuable comments by Margaret Andersen, Ronet Bachman, Loy Bilderback, Robert Broadhead, James A. Holstein, Timothy Kubal, Donileen R. Loseke, David F. Luckenbill, and Tracy M. Thibodeau. University of Delaware honors students Tammy Ader, Brian Arban, Andrew Devereaux, Thomas Madura, Karen McCready, Jacquelynn Nicnick, Meghan Shaw, Barbara Sweeney, Denise Weaver, Kelly Wesstrom, and Melissa Zwickel read the entire manuscript and gave me valuable feedback. Writing a critique of common errors in reasoning is a tricky business: it invites readers to find the mistakes in these pages. It would be nice to be able to blame scapegoats but, alas, the friends who commented on the manuscript gave me good advice—although I didn't always take it. The flaws are mine.

PREFACE TO THE UPDATED EDITION

Darrell Huff's little book, *How to Lie with Statistics,* made a bigger impression on me than anything else I read during my first year in college.[1] It wasn't even assigned reading; the TA in my statistics lab mentioned it in passing, the title struck me as amusing, and I borrowed the book from the campus library. It was a great read: by cataloging basic forms of statistical malpractice, Huff gave me a set of critical tools I could apply when reading news stories.

As the years went by, it became clear to me that the errors Huff had exposed remained alive and well. Sometime in the early 1990s, I reread *How to Lie with Statistics.* This time, I was less impressed. While Huff still offered a terrific introduction to the topic, I realized that he'd barely scratched the surface. I started thinking about writing a book of my own, one that provided a more comprehensive, more sociological approach. *Damned Lies and Statistics* was the result.

Sociology professors get used to writing for other sociologists. The chief pleasure of having written this book has been discovering the broad range of people who have read it and told me what they thought—professors and students, of course, but all sorts of folks outside academia—journalists, activists, math teachers, judges, doctors, even a mom who'd assigned it to her homeschooled child. Lots of people have found the topic interesting, and I continue to get email messages drawing my attention to particularly dubious numbers.

And there is no shortage of questionable numbers. This version of the book contains a new afterword that tries to explain why, even if we all agree that people ought to think more critically about the figures that inform our public debates, we seem unable to drive bad statistics out of the marketplace of ideas.

NOTES

1. Darrell Huff, *How to Lie with Statistics* (New York: Norton, 1954). For a symposium on Huff's book, see the special section "*How to Lie with Statistics* Turns Fifty," in *Statistical Science* 20 (2005): 205–60.

INTRODUCTION

The Worst Social Statistic Ever

The dissertation prospectus began by quoting a statistic—a "grabber" meant to capture the reader's attention. (A dissertation prospectus is a lengthy proposal for a research project leading to a Ph.D. degree—the ultimate credential for a would-be scholar.) The Graduate Student who wrote this prospectus* undoubtedly wanted to seem scholarly to the professors who would read it; they would be supervising the proposed research. And what could be more scholarly than a nice, authoritative statistic, quoted from a professional journal in the Student's field?

So the prospectus began with this (carefully footnoted) quotation: "Every year since 1950, the number of American children

---

* For reasons that will become obvious, I have decided not to name the Graduate Student, the Author, or the Journal Editor. They made mistakes, but the mistakes they made were, as this book will show, all too common.

1

gunned down has doubled." I had been invited to serve on the Student's dissertation committee. When I read the quotation, I assumed the Student had made an error in copying it. I went to the library and looked up the article the Student had cited. There, in the journal's 1995 volume, was exactly the same sentence: "Every year since 1950, the number of American children gunned down has doubled."

This quotation is my nomination for a dubious distinction: I think it may be the worst—that is, the most inaccurate—social statistic ever.

What makes this statistic so bad? Just for the sake of argument, let's assume that the "number of American children gunned down" in 1950 was one. If the number doubled each year, there must have been two children gunned down in 1951, four in 1952, eight in 1953, and so on. By 1960, the number would have been 1,024. By 1965, it would have been 32,768 (in 1965, the FBI identified only 9,960 criminal homicides in the entire country, including adult as well as child victims). In 1970, the number would have passed one million; in 1980, *one billion* (more than four times the total U.S. population in that year). Only three years later, in 1983, the number of American children gunned down would have been 8.6 billion (about twice the Earth's population at the time). Another milestone would have been passed in 1987, when the number of gunned-down American children (137 billion) would have surpassed the best estimates for the total human population throughout history (110 billion). By 1995, when the article was published, the annual number of victims would have been over *35 trillion*—a really big number, of a magnitude you rarely encounter outside economics or astronomy.

Thus my nomination: estimating the number of American child gunshot victims in 1995 at 35 trillion must be as far off—as hilariously, wildly wrong—as a social statistic can be. (If anyone spots a more inaccurate social statistic, I'd love to hear about it.)

Where did the article's Author get this statistic? I wrote the Author, who responded that the statistic came from the Children's Defense Fund (the CDF is a well-known advocacy group for children). The CDF's *The State of America's Children Yearbook—1994* does state: "The number of American children killed each year by guns has doubled since 1950."[1] Note the difference in the wording—the CDF claimed there were twice as many deaths in 1994 as in 1950; the article's Author reworded that claim and created a very different meaning.

It is worth examining the history of this statistic. It began with the CDF noting that child gunshot deaths doubled from 1950 to 1994. This is not quite as dramatic an increase as it might seem. Remember that the U.S. population also rose throughout this period; in fact, it grew about 73 percent—or nearly double. Therefore, we might expect all sorts of things—including the number of child gunshot deaths—to increase, to nearly double just because the population grew. Before we can decide whether twice as many deaths indicates that things are getting worse, we'd have to know more.* The CDF statistic raises other issues as

* For instance, since only child victims are at issue, a careful analysis would control for the relative sizes of the child population in

well: Where did the statistic come from? Who counts child gunshot deaths, and how? What do they mean by a "child" (some CDF statistics about violence include everyone under age 25)? What do they mean "killed by guns" (gunshot death statistics often include suicides and accidents, as well as homicides)? But people rarely ask questions of this sort when they encounter statistics. Most of the time, most people simply *accept statistics without question.*

Certainly, the article's Author didn't ask many probing, critical questions about the CDF's claim. Impressed by the statistic, the Author *repeated* it—well, meant to repeat it. Instead, by rewording the CDF's claim, the Author created a *mutant statistic*, one garbled almost beyond recognition.

But people treat mutant statistics just as they do other statistics—that is, they usually accept even the most implausible claims without question. For example, the Journal Editor who accepted the Author's article for publication did not bother to consider the implications of child victims doubling each year. And people repeat bad statistics: the Graduate Student copied the garbled statistic and inserted it into the dissertation prospectus. Who knows whether still other readers were impressed by the Author's statistic and remembered it or repeated it? The article remains on the shelf in hundreds of libraries, available to anyone who needs a dramatic quote. The lesson should be clear: *bad statistics live on; they take on lives of their own.*

---

the two years. We also ought to have assurances that the methods of counting child gunshot victims did not change over time, and so on.

This is a book about bad statistics, where they come from, and why they won't go away. Some statistics are born bad—they aren't much good from the start, because they are based on nothing more than guesses or dubious data. Other statistics mutate; they become bad after being mangled (as in the case of the Author's creative rewording). Either way, bad statistics are potentially important: they can be used to stir up public outrage or fear; they can distort our understanding of our world; and they can lead us to make poor policy choices.

The notion that we need to watch out for bad statistics isn't new. We've all heard people say, "You can prove anything with statistics."* My title, *Damned Lies and Statistics*, comes from a famous aphorism (usually attributed to Mark Twain or Benjamin Disraeli): "There are lies, damned lies, and statistics."[2] There is even a useful little book, still in print after more than forty years, called *How to Lie with Statistics*.[3]

Statistics, then, have a bad reputation. We suspect that statistics may be wrong, that people who use statistics may be "lying"—trying to manipulate us by using numbers to somehow distort the truth. Yet, at the same time, we need statistics; we depend upon them to summarize and clarify the nature of our complex society. This is particularly true when we talk about social problems. Debates about social problems routinely raise questions that demand statistical answers: Is the

* This is a criticism with a long history. In his book *Chartism*, published in 1840, the social critic Thomas Carlyle noted: "A witty statesman said you might prove anything with figures."

problem widespread? How many people—and which people— does it affect? Is it getting worse? What does it cost society? What will it cost to deal with it? Convincing answers to such questions demand evidence, and that usually means numbers, measurements, statistics.

But can't you prove anything with statistics? It depends on what "prove" means. If we want to know, say, how many children are "gunned down" each year, we can't simply guess—pluck a number from thin air: one hundred, one thousand, ten thousand, 35 trillion, whatever. Obviously, there's no reason to consider an arbitrary guess "proof" of anything. However, it might be possible for someone—using records kept by police departments or hospital emergency rooms or coroners—to keep track of children who have been shot; compiling careful, complete records might give us a fairly accurate idea of the number of gunned-down children. If that number seems accurate enough, we might consider it very strong evidence—or proof.

The solution to the problem of bad statistics is not to ignore all statistics, or to assume that every number is false. Some statistics are bad, but others are pretty good, and we need statistics—good statistics—to talk sensibly about social problems. The solution, then, is not to give up on statistics, but to become better judges of the numbers we encounter. We need to think critically about statistics—at least critically enough to suspect that the number of children gunned down hasn't been doubling each year since 1950.

A few years ago, the mathematician John Allen Paulos wrote *Innumeracy*, a short, readable book about "mathematical illiteracy."[4] Too few people, he argued, are comfortable with basic mathematical principles, and this makes them poor judges of the numbers they encounter. No doubt this is one reason we have so many bad statistics. But there are other reasons, as well.

Social statistics describe society, but they are also products of our social arrangements. The people who bring social statistics to our attention have reasons for doing so; they inevitably want something, just as reporters and the other media figures who repeat and publicize statistics have their own goals. Statistics are tools, used for particular purposes. Thinking critically about statistics requires understanding their place in society.

While we may be more suspicious of statistics presented by people with whom we disagree—people who favor different political parties or have different beliefs—bad statistics are used to promote all sorts of causes. Bad statistics come from conservatives on the political right and liberals on the left, from wealthy corporations and powerful government agencies, and from advocates of the poor and the powerless. In this book, I have tried to choose examples that show this range: I have selected some bad statistics used to justify causes I support, as well as others offered to promote causes I oppose. I hope that you and everyone else who reads this book will find at least one discomforting example of a bad statistic presented in behalf of a cause you support. Honesty requires that we recognize our own errors in reasoning, as well as those of our opponents.

This book can help you understand the uses of social statistics and make you better able to judge the statistics you encounter. Understanding this book will not require sophisticated mathematical knowledge. We will be talking about the most basic forms of statistics: percentages, averages, and rates—what statisticians call "descriptive statistics." These are the sorts of statistics typically addressed in the first week or so of an introductory statistics course. (The remainder of that course, like all more advanced courses in statistics, covers "inferential statistics," complex forms of reasoning that we will ignore.) This book can help you evaluate the numbers you hear on the evening news, rather than the statistical tables printed in the *American Sociological Review* and other scholarly journals. Our goal is to learn to recognize the signs of really bad statistics, so that we won't believe—let alone repeat—claims about the number of murdered children doubling each year.

1

THE IMPORTANCE OF SOCIAL STATISTICS

Nineteenth-century Americans worried about prostitution; reformers called it "*the* social evil" and warned that many women prostituted themselves. How many? For New York City alone, there were dozens of estimates: in 1833, for instance, reformers published a report declaring that there were "not less than 10,000" prostitutes in New York (equivalent to about 10 percent of the city's female population); in 1866, New York's Methodist bishop claimed there were more prostitutes (11,000 to 12,000) than Methodists in the city; other estimates for the period ranged as high as 50,000. These reformers hoped that their reports of widespread prostitution would prod the authorities to act, but city officials' most common response was to challenge the reformers' numbers. Various investigations by the police and grand juries produced their own, much lower estimates; for instance, one 1872 police report counted only 1,223 prostitutes (by that time, New York's population included nearly half a million females). Historians see a clear pattern in these cycles of competing statistics: ministers and reformers "tended to inflate statistics";[1] while "police officials tended to underestimate prostitution."[2]

Antiprostitution reformers tried to use big numbers to arouse public outrage. Big numbers meant there was a big problem: if New York had tens of thousands of prostitutes, something ought to be done. In response, the police countered that there were relatively few prostitutes—an indication that they were doing a good job. These dueling statistics resemble other, more recent debates. During Ronald Reagan's presidency, for example, activists claimed that three million Americans were homeless, while the Reagan administration insisted that the actual number of homeless people was closer to 300,000, one-tenth what the activists claimed. In other words, homeless activists argued that homelessness was a big problem that demanded additional government social programs, while the administration argued new programs were not needed to deal with what was actually a much smaller, more manageable problem. Each side presented statistics that justified its policy recommendations, and each criticized the other's numbers. The activists ridiculed the administration's figures as an attempt to cover up a large, visible problem, while the adminstration insisted that the activists' numbers were unrealistic exaggerations.[3]

Statistics, then, can become weapons in political struggles over social problems and social policy. Advocates of different positions use numbers to make their points ("It's a big problem!"

"No, it's not!"). And, as the example of nineteenth-century estimates of prostitution reminds us, statistics have been used as weapons for some time.

THE RISE OF SOCIAL STATISTICS

In fact, the first "statistics" were meant to influence debates over social issues. The term acquired its modern meaning—numeric evidence—in the 1830s, around the time that New York reformers estimated that the city had 10,000 prostitutes. The forerunner of statistics was called "political arithmetic"; these studies—mostly attempts to calculate population size and life expectancy—emerged in seventeenth-century Europe, particularly in England and France. Analysts tried to count births, deaths, and marriages because they believed that a growing population was evidence of a healthy *state;* those who conducted such numeric studies—as well as other, nonquantitative analyses of social and political prosperity—came to be called *statists.* Over time, the statists' social research led to the new term for quantitative evidence: *statistics.*[4]

Early social researchers believed that information about society could help governments devise wise policies. They were well aware of the scientific developments of their day and, like other scientists, they came to value accuracy and objectivity. Counting—quantifying—offered a way of making their studies more precise, and let them concisely summarize lots of information.

Over time, social research became less theoretical and more quantitative. As the researchers collected and analyzed their data, they began to see patterns. From year to year, they discovered, the numbers of births, deaths, and even marriages remained relatively stable; this stability suggested that social arrangements had an underlying order, that what happened in a society depended on more than simply its government's recent actions, and analysts began paying more attention to underlying social conditions.

By the beginning of the nineteenth century, the social order seemed especially threatened: cities were larger than ever before; economies were beginning to industrialize; and revolutions in America and France had made it clear that political stability could not be taken for granted. The need for information, for facts that could guide social policy, was greater than ever before. A variety of government agencies began collecting and publishing statistics: the United States and several European countries began conducting regular censuses to collect population statistics; courts, prisons, and police began keeping track of the numbers of crimes and criminals; physicians kept records of patients; educators counted students; and so on. Scholars organized statistical societies to share the results of their studies and to discuss the best methods for gathering and interpreting statistics. And reformers who sought to confront the nineteenth-century's many social problems—the impoverished and the diseased, the fallen woman and the child laborer, the factory workforce and dispossessed agricultural labor—found statistics useful in demonstrating the extent and severity of suffering. Statistics gave both government officials and reformers hard evidence—proof that what they said was true. Numbers offered a kind of precision: instead of talking about prostitution as a vaguely defined problem, reformers began to make specific, numeric claims (for example, that New York had 10,000 prostitutes).

During the nineteenth century, then, statistics—numeric statements about social life—became an authoritative way to describe social problems. There was growing respect for science, and statistics offered a way to bring the authority of science to debates about social policy. In fact, this had been the main goal of the first statisticians—they wanted to study society through counting and use the resulting numbers to influence social policy. They succeeded; statistics gained widespread acceptance as the best way to measure social problems. Today, statistics continue to play a central role in our efforts to understand these problems. But, beginning in the nineteenth century and continuing through today, social statistics have had two purposes, one public, the other often hidden. Their public purpose is to give an accurate, true description of society. But people also use statistics to support particular views about social problems. Numbers are created and repeated because they supply ammunition for political struggles, and this political purpose is often hidden behind assertions that numbers, simply because they are numbers, must be correct. People use statistics to support particular points of view, and it is naive simply to accept numbers as accurate, without examining who is using them and why.

CREATING SOCIAL PROBLEMS

We tend to think of social problems as harsh realities, like gravity or earthquakes, that exist completely independent of human action. But the very term reveals that this is incorrect: *social problems are products of what people do*.

This is true in two senses. First, we picture social problems as snarls or flaws in the social fabric. Social problems have their causes in society's arrangements; when some women turn to prostitution or some individuals have no homes, we assume that society has failed (although we may disagree over whether that failure involves not providing enough jobs, or not giving children proper moral instruction, or something else). Most people understand that social problems are social in this sense.

But there is a second reason social problems are social. Someone has to bring these problems to our attention, to give them names, describe their causes and characteristics, and so on. Sociologists speak of social problems being "constructed"— that is, created or assembled through the actions of activists, officials, the news media, and other people who draw attention to particular problems.[5] "Social problem" is a label we give to some social conditions, and it is that label that turns a condition we take for granted into something we consider troubling. This means that the processes of identifying and publicizing social problems are important. When we start thinking of prostitution or homelessness as a social problem, we are responding to campaigns by reformers who seek to arouse our concern about the issue.

The creation of a new social problem can be seen as a sort of public drama, a play featuring a fairly standard cast of characters. Often, the leading roles are played by *social activists*—individuals dedicated to promoting a cause, to making others aware of the problem. Activists draw attention to new social problems by holding protest demonstrations, attracting media coverage, recruiting new members to their cause, lobbying officials to do something about the situation, and so on. They are the most obvious, the most visible participants in creating awareness of social problems.

Successful activists attract support from others. The *mass media*—including both the press (reporters for newspapers or television news programs) and entertainment media (such as television talk shows)—relay activists' claims to the general public. Reporters often find it easy to turn those claims into interesting news stories; after all, a new social problem is a fresh topic, and it may affect lots of people, pose dramatic threats, and lead to proposals to change the lives of those involved. Media coverage, especially sympathetic coverage, can make millions of people aware of and concerned about a social problem. Activists need the media to provide that coverage, just as the media depend on activists and other sources for news to report.

Often activists also enlist the support of *experts*—doctors, scientists, economists, and so on—who presumably have special qualifications to talk about the causes and consequences of some social problem. Experts may have done research on the problem and can report their findings. Activists use experts to make claims about social problems seem authoritative, and the mass media often rely on experts' testimonies to make news stories about a new problem seem more convincing. In turn, experts enjoy the respectful attention they receive from activists and the media.[6]

Not all social problems are promoted by struggling, independent activists; creating new social problems is sometimes the work of powerful organizations and institutions. *Government officials* who promote problems range from prominent politicians trying to arouse concern in order to create election campaign issues, to anonymous bureaucrats proposing that their agencies' programs be expanded to solve some social problem. And *businesses, foundations, and other private organizations* sometimes have their own reasons to promote particular social issues. Public and private organizations usually command the resources needed to organize effective campaigns to create social problems. They can afford to hire experts to conduct research, to sponsor and encourage activists, and to publicize their causes in ways that attract media attention.[7]

In other words, when we become aware of—and start to worry about—some new social problem, our concern is usually the result of efforts by some combination of *problem promoters*—activists, reporters, experts, officials, or private organizations—who have worked to create the sense that this is an important problem, one that deserves our attention. In this sense, people deliberately construct social problems.*

*I am not implying that there is anything wrong with calling attention to social problems. In fact, this book can be seen as my

Efforts to create or promote social problems, particularly when they begin to attract attention, may inspire opposition. Sometimes this involves officials responding to critics by defending existing policies as adequate. Recall that New York police minimized the number of prostitutes in the city, just as the Reagan administration argued that activists exaggerated the number of homeless persons. In other cases, opposition comes from private interests; for example, the Tobacco Institute (funded by the tobacco industry) became notorious for, over decades, challenging every research finding that smoking was harmful.

Statistics play an important role in campaigns to create—or defuse claims about—new social problems. Most often, such statistics describe the problem's size: there are 10,000 prostitutes in New York City, or three million homeless people. When social problems first come to our attention, perhaps in a televised news report, we're usually given an example or two (perhaps video footage of homeless individuals living on city streets) and then a statistical estimate (of the number of homeless people). Typically this is a big number. Big numbers warn us that the problem is a common one, compelling our attention, concern, and action. The media like to report statistics because numbers seem to be "hard facts"—little nuggets of indisputable truth. Activists trying to draw media attention to a new social problem often find that the press demands statistics: reporters insist on getting estimates of

_____

effort to construct "bad statistics" as a problem that ought to concern people.

the problem's size—how many people are affected, how much it costs, and so on. Experts, officials, and private organizations commonly report having studied the problem, and they present statistics based on their research. Thus, the key players in creating new social problems all have reason to present statistics.

In virtually every case, promoters use statistics as ammunition; they choose numbers that will draw attention to or away from a problem, arouse or defuse public concern. People use statistics to support their point of view, to bring others around to their way of thinking. Activists trying to gain recognition for what they believe is a big problem will offer statistics that seem to prove that the problem is indeed a big one (and they may choose to downplay, ignore, or dispute any statistics that might make it seem smaller). The media favor disturbing statistics about big problems because big problems make more interesting, more compelling news, just as experts' research (and the experts themselves) seem more important if their subject is a big, important problem. These concerns lead people to present statistics that support their position, their cause, their interests. There is an old expression that captures this tendency: "Figures may not lie, but liars figure." Certainly we need to understand that people debating social problems choose statistics selectively and present them to support their points of view. Gun-control advocates will be more likely to report the number of children killed by guns, while opponents of gun control will prefer to count citizens who use guns to defend themselves from attack. Both numbers may be correct, but most people debating gun control present only the statistic that bolsters their position.[8]

THE PUBLIC AS AN INNUMERATE AUDIENCE

Most claims drawing attention to new social problems aim to persuade all of us—that is, the members of the general public. We are the audience, or at least one important audience, for statistics and other claims about social problems. If the public becomes convinced that prostitution or homelessness is a serious problem, then something is more likely to be done: officials will take action, new policies will begin, and so on. Therefore, campaigns to create social problems use statistics to help arouse the public's concern.

This is not difficult. The general public tends to be receptive to claims about new social problems, and we rarely think critically about social problems statistics. Recall that the media like to report statistics because numbers seem to be factual, little nuggets of truth. The public tends to agree; we usually treat statistics as facts.

In part, this is because we are innumerate. Innumeracy is the mathematical equivalent of illiteracy; it is "an inability to deal comfortably with the fundamental notions of number and chance."[9] Just as some people cannot read or read poorly, many people have trouble thinking clearly about numbers.

One common innumerate error involves not distinguishing among large numbers. A very small child may be pleased by the gift of a penny; a slightly older child understands that a penny or even a dime can't buy much, but a dollar can buy some things, ten dollars considerably more, and a hundred dollars a great deal (at least from a child's point of view). Most adults clearly grasp what one can do with a hundred, a thousand, ten thousand, even one hundred thousand dollars, but then our imaginations begin to fail us. Big numbers blend together: a million, a billion, a trillion—what's the difference? They're all big numbers. (Actually, of course, there are tremendous differences. The difference between a million and a billion is the difference between one dollar and one thousand dollars; the difference between a million and a trillion is the difference between one dollar and a million dollars.)

Because many people have trouble appreciating the differences among big numbers, they tend to uncritically accept social statistics (which often, of course, feature big numbers). What does it matter, they may say, whether there are 300,000 homeless or 3,000,000?—either way, it's a big number. They'd never make this mistake dealing with smaller numbers; everyone understands that it makes a real difference whether there'll be three people or thirty coming by tomorrow night for dinner. A difference (thirty is ten times greater than three) that seems obvious with smaller, more familiar numbers gets blurred when we deal with bigger numbers (3,000,000 is ten times greater than 300,000). If society is going to feed the homeless, having an accurate count is just as important as it is for an individual planning to host three—or thirty—dinner guests.

Innumeracy—widespread confusion about basic mathematical ideas—means that many statistical claims about social problems don't get the critical attention they deserve. This is not simply because an innumerate public is being manipulated by advocates who cynically promote inaccurate statistics. Often, statistics about social problems originate with sincere, well-meaning people who are themselves innumerate; they may not grasp the full implications of what they are saying. Similarly, the media are not immune to innumeracy; reporters commonly repeat the figures their sources give them without bothering to think critically about them.

The result can be a social comedy. Activists want to draw attention to a problem—prostitution, homelessness, or whatever. The press asks the activists for statistics—How many prostitutes? How many homeless? Knowing that big numbers indicate big problems and knowing that it will be hard to get action unless people can be convinced a big problem exists (and sincerely believing that there is a big problem), the activists produce a big estimate, and the press, having no good way to check the number, simply publicizes it. The general public—most of us suffering from at least a mild case of innumeracy—tends to accept the figure without question. After all, it's a big number, and there's no real difference among big numbers.

ORGANIZATIONAL PRACTICES
AND OFFICIAL STATISTICS

One reason we tend to accept statistics uncritically is that we assume that numbers come from experts who know what they're doing. Often these experts work for government agencies, such as the U.S. Bureau of the Census, and producing statistics is part of their job. Data that come from the government—crime rates, unemployment rates, poverty rates—are *official statistics*.[10] There is a natural tendency to treat these figures as straightforward facts that cannot be questioned.

This ignores the way statistics are produced. All statistics, even the most authoritative, are created by people. This does not mean that they are inevitably flawed or wrong, but it does mean that we ought to ask ourselves just how the statistics we encounter were created.

Let's say a couple decides to get married. This requires going to a government office, taking out a marriage license, and having whoever conducts the marriage ceremony sign and file the license. Periodically, officials add up the number of marriage licenses filed and issue a report on the number of marriages. This is a relatively straightforward bit of recordkeeping, but notice that the accuracy of marriage statistics depends on couples' willingness to cooperate with the procedures. For example, imagine a couple who decide to "get married" without taking out a license; they might even have a wedding ceremony, yet their marriage will not be counted in the official record. Or consider couples that cohabit—live together—without getting married; there is no official record of their living arrangement. And there is the added problem of recordkeeping: is the system for filing, recording, and generally keeping track of marriages accurate, or do mistakes occur? These examples remind us that the official number of marriages reflects certain bureaucratic decisions about what will be counted and how to do the counting.

Now consider a more complicated example: statistics on suicide. Typically, a coroner decides which deaths are suicides. This can be relatively straightforward: perhaps the dead individual left behind a note clearly stating an intent to commit suicide. But often there is no note, and the coroner must gather evidence that points to suicide—perhaps the deceased is known to have been depressed, the death occurred in a locked house, the cause of death was an apparently self-inflicted gunshot to the head, and so on. There are two potential mistakes here. The first is that the coroner may label a death a "suicide" when, in fact, there was another cause (in mystery novels, at least, murder often is disguised as suicide). The second possibility for error is that the coroner may assign another cause of death to what was, in fact, a suicide. This is probably a greater risk, because some people who kill themselves want to conceal that fact (for example, some single-car automobile fatalities are suicides designed to look like accidents so that the individual's family can avoid embarrassment or collect life insurance benefits). In addition, surviving family members may be ashamed by a relative's suicide, and they may press the coroner to assign another cause of death, such as accident.

In other words, official records of suicide reflect coroners' judgments about the causes of death in what can be ambiguous circumstances. The act of suicide tends to be secretive—it usually occurs in private—and the motives of the dead cannot always be known. Labeling some deaths as "suicides" and others as "homicides," "accidents," or whatever will sometimes be wrong, although we cannot know exactly how often. Note, too, that individual coroners may assess cases differently; we might imagine one coroner who is relatively willing to label deaths suicides, and another who is very reluctant to do so. Presented with the same set of cases, the first coroner might find many more suicides than the second.[11]

It is important to appreciate that coroners view their task as classifying individual deaths, as giving each one an appropriate label, rather than as compiling statistics for suicide rates. Whatever statistical reports come out of coroners' offices (say, total number of suicides in the jurisdiction during the past year) are by-products of their real work (classifying individual deaths). That is, coroners are probably more concerned with being able to justify their decisions in individual cases than they are with whatever overall statistics emerge from those decisions.

The example of suicide records reveals that all official statistics are products—and often by-products—of decisions by various officials: not just coroners, but also the humble clerks who fill out and file forms, the exalted supervisors who prepare summary reports, and so on. These people make choices (and sometimes errors) that shape whatever statistics finally emerge from their organization or agency, and the organization provides a context for those choices. For example, the law requires coroners to choose among a specified set of causes for death: homicide, suicide, accident, natural causes, and so on. That list of causes reflects our culture. Thus, our laws do not allow coroners to list "witchcraft" as a cause of death, although that might be considered a reasonable choice in other societies. We can imagine different laws that would give coroners different arrays of choices: perhaps there might be no category for suicide; perhaps people who kill themselves might be considered ill, and their deaths listed as occurring from natural causes; or perhaps suicides might be grouped with homicides in a single category of deaths caused by humans. In other words, official statistics reflect what sociologists call *organizational practices*—the organization's culture and structure shape officials' actions, and those actions determine whatever statistics finally emerge.

Now consider an even more complicated example. Police officers have a complex job; they must maintain order, enforce the law, and assist citizens in a variety of ways. Unlike the coroner who faces a relatively short list of choices in assigning cause of death, the police have to make all sorts of decisions. For example, police responding to a call about a domestic dispute (say, a fight between husband and wife) have several, relatively ill-defined options. Perhaps they should arrest someone; perhaps the wife wants her husband arrested—or perhaps she says she does not want that to happen; perhaps the officers ought to encourage the couple to separate for the night; perhaps they ought to offer to take the wife to a women's shelter; perhaps they ought to try talking to the couple to calm them down; perhaps they find that talking doesn't work, and then pick arrest or a shelter as a second choice; perhaps they decide that the dispute has already been settled, or that there is really nothing wrong. Police must make decisions about how to respond in such cases, and some—but probably not all—of those choices will be reflected in official statistics. If officers make an arrest, the incident will be recorded in arrest statistics, but if the officers decide to deal with the incident informally (by talking with the couple until they calm down), there may be no statistical record of what happens. The choices officers make depend on many factors. If the domestic dispute call comes near the end of the officers' shift, they may favor quick solutions. If their department has a new policy to crack down on domestic disputes, officers will be more likely to make arrests. All these decisions, each shaped by various considerations, will affect whatever statistics eventually summarize the officers' actions.[12]

Like our earlier examples of marriage records and coroners labeling suicides, the example of police officers dealing with domestic disputes reveals that officials make decisions (relatively straightforward for marriage records, more complicated for coroners, and far less clear-cut in the case of the police), that official statistics are by-products of those decisions (police officers probably give even less thought than coroners to the statistical outcomes of their decisions), and that organizational practices form the context for those decisions (while there may be relatively little variation in how marriage records are kept, organizational practices likely differ more among coroners' offices, and there is great variation in how police deal with their complex decisions, with differences among departments, precincts, officers, and so on). In short, even official statistics are social products, shaped by the people and organizations that create them.

THINKING ABOUT STATISTICS AS SOCIAL PRODUCTS

The lesson should be clear: statistics—even official statistics such as crime rates, unemployment rates, and census counts—

are products of social activity. We sometimes talk about statistics as though they are facts that simply exist, like rocks, completely independent of people, and that people gather statistics much as rock collectors pick up stones. This is wrong. All statistics are created through people's actions: people have to decide what to count and how to count it, people have to do the counting and the other calculations, and people have to interpret the resulting statistics, to decide what the numbers mean. All statistics are social products, the results of people's efforts.

Once we understand this, it becomes clear that we should not simply accept statistics by uncritically treating numbers as true or factual. If people create statistics, then those numbers need to be assessed, evaluated. Some statistics are pretty good; they reflect people's best efforts to measure social problems carefully, accurately, and objectively. But other numbers are bad statistics—figures that may be wrong, even wildly wrong. We need to be able to sort out the good statistics from the bad. There are three basic questions that deserve to be asked whenever we encounter a new statistic.

1. *Who created this statistic?* Every statistic has its authors, its creators. Sometimes a number comes from a particular individual. On other occasions, large organizations (such as the Bureau of the Census) claim authorship (although each statistic undoubtedly reflects the work of particular people within the organization).

In asking who the creators are, we ought to be less concerned with the names of the particular individuals who produced a number than with their part in the public drama about statistics.

Does a particular statistic come from activists, who are striving to draw attention to and arouse concern about a social problem? Is the number being reported by the media in an effort to prove that this problem is newsworthy? Or does the figure come from officials, bureaucrats who routinely keep track of some social phenomenon, and who may not have much stake in what the numbers show?

2. *Why was this statistic created?* The identities of the people who create statistics are often clues to their motives. In general, activists seek to promote their causes, to draw attention to social problems. Therefore, we can suspect that they will favor large numbers, be more likely to produce them and less likely to view them critically. When reformers cry out that there are many prostitutes or homeless individuals, we need to recognize that their cause might seem less compelling if their numbers were smaller. On the other hand, note that other people may favor lower numbers. Remember that New York police officials produced figures showing that there were very few prostitutes in the city as evidence they were doing a good job. We need to be aware that the people who produce statistics often care what the numbers show, they use numbers as tools of persuasion.

3. *How was this statistic created?* We should not discount a statistic simply because its creators have a point of view, because they view a social problem as more or less serious. Rather, we need to ask how they arrived at the statistic. All statistics are imperfect, but some are far less perfect than others. There is a big difference between a number produced by a wild guess, and one generated through carefully designed research. This is the key

question. Once we understand that all social statistics are created by someone, and that everyone who creates social statistics wants to prove something (even if that is only that they are careful, reliable, and unbiased), it becomes clear that the methods of creating statistics are key. The remainder of this book focuses on this third question.

PLAN OF THE BOOK

The following chapters discuss some of the most common and important problems with the creation and interpretation of social statistics. Chapter 2 examines four basic sources of bad statistics: bad guesses, deceptive definitions, confusing questions, and biased samples. Chapter 3 looks at mutant statistics, at ways even good statistics can be mangled, misused, and misunderstood. Chapter 4 discusses the logic of statistical comparison and explores some of the most common errors in comparing two or more time periods, places, groups, or social problems. Chapter 5 considers debates over statistics. Finally, chapter 6 examines three general approaches to thinking about statistics.

2

SOFT FACTS

Sources of Bad Statistics

A child advocate tells Congress that 3,000 children per year are lured with Internet messages and then kidnapped. Tobacco opponents attribute over 400,000 deaths per year to smoking. Antihunger activists say that 31 million Americans regularly "face hunger." Although the press tends to present such statistics as facts, someone, somehow, had to produce these numbers. But how? Is there some law enforcement agency that keeps track of which kidnappings begin with online seductions? Are there medical authorities who decide which lung cancer deaths are caused by smoking, and which have other causes, such as breathing polluted air? Who counts Americans facing hunger—and what does "facing hunger" mean, anyway?

Chapter 1 argued that people produce statistics. Of course they do. All human knowledge—including statistics—is created through people's actions; everything we know is shaped by our language, culture, and society. Sociologists call this the *social construction of knowledge.* Saying that knowledge is socially constructed does not mean that all we know is somehow fanciful, arbitrary, flawed, or wrong. For example, scientific knowledge can be remarkably accurate, so accurate that we may forget the people and social processes that produced it. I'm writing this chapter on a computer that represents the accumulation of centuries of scientific knowledge. Designing and building this computer required that people come to understand principles of physics, chemistry, electrical engineering, computer science—who knows what else? The development of that knowledge was a social process, yet the fact that the computer works reliably reflects the great confidence we have in the knowledge that went into building it.

This is one way to think about facts. Knowledge is factual when evidence supports it and we have great confidence in its accuracy. What we call "hard fact" is information supported by strong, convincing evidence; this means evidence that, so far as we know, we cannot deny, however we examine or test it. Facts always can be questioned, but they hold up under questioning. How did people come by this information? How did they interpret it? Are other interpretations possible? The more satisfactory the answers to such questions, the "harder" the facts.

Our knowledge about society tends to be "softer" than our knowledge of the physical world. Physicists have far more confidence in their measurements of the atomic weight of mercury than sociologists have in their descriptions of public attitudes toward abortion. This is because there are well-established, generally agreed-upon procedures for measuring atomic weights and because such measurements consistently produce the same results. In contrast, there is less agreement among social scientists about how best to measure—or even how to define—public opinion.

Although we sometimes treat social statistics as straightforward, hard facts, we ought to ask how those numbers are created. Remember that people promoting social problems want to persuade others, and they use statistics to make their claims more persuasive. Often, the ways people produce statistics are flawed: their numbers may be little more than guesses; or the figures may be a product of poor definitions, flawed measurements, or weak sampling. These are the four basic ways to create bad social statistics.

GUESSING

Activists hoping to draw attention to a new social problem often find that there are no good statistics available.* When a trouble-

*While activists are particularly likely to face this problem (because they often are the first to try to bring a problem to public attention), anyone trying to promote a new social problem—including experts, officials, and those representing the media or other institutions—may have the same difficulties. Just as I sometimes use the general terms "advocates" or "promoters" to refer to all the sorts of people who help create social problems, I use "activists" to suggest that they are the ones especially—but not uniquely—likely to handle statistics in particular ways.

some social condition has been ignored, there usually are no accurate records about the condition to serve as the basis for good statistics. Therefore, when reporters ask activists for facts and figures ("Exactly how big is this problem?"), the activists cannot produce official, authoritative numbers.

What activists do have is their own sense that the problem is widespread and getting worse. After all, they believe it is an important problem, and they spend much of their time learning more about it and talking to other people who share their concerns. A hothouse atmosphere develops in which everyone agrees this is a big, important problem. People tell one another stories about the problem and, if no one has been keeping careful records, activists soon realize that many cases of the problem—maybe the vast majority—go unreported and leave no records.

Criminologists use the expression "the dark figure" to refer to the proportion of crimes that don't appear in crime statistics.[1] In theory, citizens report crimes to the police, the police keep records of those reports, and those records become the basis for calculating crime rates. But some crimes are not reported (because people are too afraid or too busy to call the police, or because they doubt the police will be able to do anything useful), and the police may not keep records of all the reports they receive, so the crime rate inevitably underestimates the actual amount of crime. The difference between the number of officially recorded crimes and the true number of crimes is the dark figure.

Every social problem has a dark figure because some instances (of crime, child abuse, poverty, or whatever) inevitably go unrecorded. How big is the dark figure? When we first learn about a problem that has never before received attention, when no one has any idea how common the problem actually is, we might think of the dark figure as being the entire problem. In other cases where recordkeeping is very thorough, the dark figure may be relatively small (for example, criminologists believe that the vast majority of homicides are recorded, simply because dead bodies usually come to police attention).

So, when reporters or officials ask activists about the size of a newly created social problem, the activists usually have to guess about the problem's dark figure. They offer estimates, educated guesses, guesstimates, ballpark figures, or stabs in the dark. When *Nightline*'s Ted Koppel asked Mitch Snyder, a leading activist for the homeless in the early 1980s, for the source of the estimate that there were two to three million homeless persons, Snyder explained: "Everybody demanded it. Everybody said we want a number. . . . We got on the phone, we made a lot of calls, we talked to a lot of people, and we said, 'Okay, here are some numbers.' They have no meaning, no value."[2] Because activists sincerely believe that the new problem is big and important, and because they suspect that there is a very large dark figure of unreported or unrecorded cases, the *activists' estimates tend to be high*, to err on the side of exaggeration. Their guesses are far more likely to overestimate than underestimate a problem's size. (Activists also favor round numbers. It is remarkable how often their estimates peg the frequency of some social problem at one [or two or more] million cases per year.[3])

Being little more than guesses—and probably guesses that are too high—usually will not discredit activists' estimates. After all, the media ask activists for estimates precisely because they can't find more accurate statistics. Reporters want to report facts, activists' numbers look like facts, and it may be difficult, even impossible to find other numbers, so the media tend to report the activists' figures. (Scott Adams, the cartoonist who draws *Dilbert,* explains the process: "Reporters are faced with the daily choice of painstakingly researching stories or writing whatever people tell them. Both approaches pay the same."[4])

Once a number appears in one news report, that report is a potential source for everyone who becomes interested in the social problem; officials, experts, activists, and other reporters routinely repeat figures that appear in press reports. *The number takes on a life of its own, and it goes through "number launder-ing."*[5] Its origins as someone's best guess are now forgotten and, through repetition, it comes to be treated as a straightforward fact—accurate and authoritative. Soon the trail becomes muddy. People lose track of the estimate's original source, but they assume the number must be correct because it appears every-where—in news reports, politicians' speeches, articles in schol-arly journals and law reviews, and so on. Over time, as people repeat the number, they may begin to change its meaning, to embellish the statistic.

Consider early estimates for the crime of stalking.[6] Concern about stalking spread very rapidly in the early 1990s; the media publicized the problem, and most state legislatures passed anti-stalking laws. At that time, no official agencies were keeping track of stalking cases, and no studies of the extent of stalking had been done, so there was no way anyone could know how often stalking occurred. After a newsmagazine story reported "researchers suggest that up to 200,000 people exhibit a stalker's traits,"[7] other news reports picked up the "suggested" figure and confidently repeated that there were 200,000 people being stalked. Soon, the media began to improve the statistic. The host of a television talk show declared, "There are an estimated 200,000 stalkers in the United States, and those are only the ones that we have track of."[8] An article in *Cosmopolitan* warned: "Some two hundred thousand people in the U.S. pursue the famous. No one knows how many people stalk the rest of us, but the figure is probably higher."[9] Thus, the original guess became a foundation for other, even bigger guesses (chapter 3 explores how repeating statistics often alters their meaning).[10]

People who create or repeat a statistic often feel they have a stake in defending the number. When someone disputes an estimate and offers a very different (often lower) figure, people may rush to defend the original estimate and attack the new number and anyone who dares to use it. For example, after activists estimated that there were three million homeless in the early 1980s and the Reagan administration countered that the actual number was closer to 300,000, the activists argued that the administration's figures could not be trusted: after all, the administration was committed to reducing expenditures on social programs and could be expected to minimize the need for additional social services.[11] Various social scientists set out to measure the size of the homeless population. When their findings confirmed that the 300,000 figure was more reasonable, the social scientists came under attack from activists who charged that the research had to be flawed, that the researchers' sympathies must have been with the administration, not the homeless.[12] In general, the press continued reporting the large estimates. After all, activists and reporters knew that the actual number of homeless persons was much higher—didn't everyone agree that three million was the correct figure? This example suggests that *any estimate can be defended by challenging the motives of anyone who disputes the figure.*

In addition, *the dark figure often plays a prominent part in defending guesses.* There are always some hidden, unnoticed, uncounted cases and, because they are uncounted, we cannot know just how many there are. Arguing that the dark figure is large, perhaps very large ("The cases we know about are just the tip of the iceberg!"), makes any estimate seem possible, even reasonable. We know that some victims do not report rapes, but what proportion of rapes goes unreported? Is it two in three? Surveys that ask people whether they've been victimized by a crime and, if so, whether they reported the crime to the police, find that about two-thirds of all rapes go unreported.[13] But surely these surveys are imperfect; some rape victims undoubtedly refuse to tell the interviewer they've been victimized, so there still must be a dark figure. Some antirape activists argue that the dark figure of unreported rapes is very large, that only one rape in ten gets reported (this would mean that, for every two victims who fail to report their attacks to the police but tell an interviewer about the crimes, seven others refuse to confide in the interviewer).[14] Such arguments make an impassioned defense of any guess possible.

Activists are by no means the only people who make statistical guesses. It is difficult to count users of illicit drugs (who of course try to conceal their drug use), but government agencies charged with enforcing drug laws face demands for such statistics. Many of the numbers they present—estimates for the number of addicts, the amounts addicts steal, the volume of illicit drugs produced in different countries, and so on—cannot bear close inspection. They are basically guesses and, because having a big drug problem makes the agencies' work seem more important, the officials' guesses tend to exaggerate the problem's size.[15] It makes little difference whether those promoting social problems are activists or officials: when it is difficult to measure a social problem accurately, guessing offers a solution; and there usually are advantages to guessing high.

There is nothing terribly wrong with guessing what the size of a social problem might be. Often we can't know the true extent of a problem. Making an educated guess—and making it clear that it's just someone's best guess—gives us a starting point. The real trouble begins when people begin treating the guess as a fact, repeating the figure, forgetting how it came into being, embellishing it, developing an emotional stake in its promotion and survival, and attacking those who dare to question what was, remember, originally just someone's best guess. Unfortunately, this process occurs all too often when social problems first come to public attention, because at that stage, a guess may be all anyone has got.

DEFINING

Any attempt to talk about a social problem has to involve some sort of definition, some answer to the question: "What is the nature of this problem?" The definition can be—and often is—vague; sometimes it is little more than an example. For instance, a television news story may tell us about a particular child who was beaten to death, and then say, "This is an example of child abuse." The example takes the place of a precise definition of the problem. One difficulty with this practice is that media coverage usually features dramatic, especially disturbing examples because they make the story more compelling. Using the worst case to characterize a social problem encourages us to view that case as typical and to think about the problem in extreme terms. This distorts our understanding of the problem. Relatively few cases of child abuse involve fatal beatings; comparatively mundane cases of neglect are far more common. But defining child abuse through examples of fatal beatings can shape how we think about the problem, and child-protection policies designed to prevent fatalities may not be the best way to protect children from neglect. *Whenever examples substitute for definitions, there is a risk that our understanding of the problem will be distorted.*

Of course, not all definitions of social problems depend on dramatic examples. People promoting social problems sometimes do offer definitions. When they do so, they tend to prefer general, broad, inclusive definitions. Broad definitions encompass more cases—and more kinds of cases. Suppose we want to define sexual violence. Certainly our definition should include rapes. But what about attempted rapes—should they be included? Does being groped or fondled count? What about seeing a stranger briefly expose himself? A narrow definition—say, "sexual violence is forcible sexual contact involving penetration"—will include far fewer cases than a broad definition—for example, "sexual violence is any uninvited sexual action."[16] This has obvious implications for social statistics because *broad definitions support much larger estimates of a problem's size.**

No definition of a social problem is perfect, but there are two principal ways such definitions can be flawed. On the one hand, we may worry that a definition is too broad, that it encompasses more than it ought to include. That is, broad definitions identify some cases as part of the problem that we might think ought not to be included; statisticians call such cases *false positives* (that is, they mistakenly identify cases as part of the problem). On the other hand, a definition that is too narrow excludes cases that we might think ought to be included; these are *false negatives* (incorrectly identified as not being part of the problem).[17]

In general, *activists trying to create a new social problem view false negatives as more troubling than false positives.* Remember that activists often feel frustrated because they want to get people concerned about some social condition that has been

---

*Activists often couple big statistics based on broad definitions with compelling examples of the most serious cases. For example, claims about child abuse might feature the case of a murdered child as a typical example, yet offer a statistical estimate that includes millions of less serious instances of abuse and neglect.

ignored. The general failure to recognize and acknowledge that something is wrong is part of what the activists want to correct; therefore, they may be especially careful not to make things worse themselves by defining the problem too narrowly. A definition that is too narrow fails to recognize the problem's full extent; in doing so, it continues ignoring at least a part of the harm and suffering that ought to be recognized. Thus, activists might point to an example of a woman traumatized by a flasher exposing himself, and then argue that the definition of sexual violence needs to be broad enough to acknowledge the harm suffered by that woman. Activists sometimes favor definitions broad enough to encompass every case that ought to be included; that is, they promote broad definitions in hopes of eliminating all false negatives. Remember, too, that broad definitions make it easier to justify the big numbers advocates prefer.

However, broad definitions invite criticism. Not everyone finds it helpful to lump rape and flashing into a single category of sexual violence. Such broad definitions obscure important differences within the category: rape and flashing both may be unwanted, but classifying them together may imply they are equally serious. Worse, broad definitions encompass cases that not everyone considers instances of social problems; that is, while they minimize false negatives, they do so at the cost of maximizing cases that critics may see as false positives. Consider the long-running debate over the definition of pornography.[18] What ought to be considered pornographic? Presumably hardcore videos of people having sex are included in virtually all definitions. But is *Playboy* pornographic? What about nude sculptures, or the annual *Sports Illustrated* swimsuit issue? Some antipornography activists may favor a very broad, inclusive definition, while their critics may argue that such definitions are too broad ("*That's* not pornography!").

Clearly, the definition of a social problem will affect statistics about that problem. The broader the definition, the easier it is to justify large estimates for a problem's extent. When someone announces that millions of Americans are illiterate, it is important to ask how that announcement defines illiteracy.[19] Some might assume that illiteracy means that a person cannot read or write at all, but the speaker may be referring to "functional illiteracy" (that is, the inability to read a newspaper or a map or to fill out a job application or an income tax form). Does illiterate mean not reading at all? Not reading at the third-grade level? Not reading at the sixth-grade level? Defining illiteracy narrowly (as being unable to read at all) will include far fewer people and therefore produce far lower statistical estimates than a broad definition (being unable to read at the sixth-grade level).

Often, definitions include multiple elements, each of which can serve to make the definition broader or narrower. Consider homelessness again. What should a definition of homelessness encompass? Should it include the *cause* of homelessness? If a tornado destroys a neighborhood and the residents have to be housed in temporary emergency shelters, are they homeless, or should we count only people whose poverty makes them homeless? What about the length of *time* spent homeless? Does someone who spends a single night on the streets count, or should the label "homeless" be restricted to those who spend several (and if so, how many?) nights on the streets? Each element in the definition makes a difference. If we're counting homeless persons, and we count only those whose poverty made them homeless, we'll find fewer than if we include disaster victims. If we count those who were without a home for thirty days in the last year, we will find fewer homeless people than if our standard is only ten days, and using ten as a standard will produce a lower number than if we agree that even a single night on the streets qualifies someone to be considered homeless.

In fact, some advocates for the homeless argue that definitions based on these elements are far too narrow, and they offer even broader definitions.[20] They suggest that people who stay in the homes of friends or relatives—but who have no homes of their own—ought to be counted as homeless. Under this definition, an impoverished mother and child who never spend a night on the streets or in a shelter but who "double up" and live with relatives or another poor family ought to be counted as homeless. Obviously, using this broader standard to count cases will produce higher numbers than definitions that restrict homelessness to those living on the streets. Still other advocates argue that people whose housing is inadequate or insufficient also ought to be counted as homeless. This still broader definition will lead to even larger numbers. Calculating the number of homeless people (or illiterate people or acts of sexual violence) inevitably reflects our definitions.

In other words, statistics about social problems always depend on how we define the problem. The broader the definition, the bigger the statistic. And, because people promoting social problems favor big numbers (because they make the problem seem bigger and more important), we can expect that they will favor broad definitions. Often, advocates justify broad definitions by emphasizing the importance of being inclusive. People who spend a single night on the streets (or who have to stay with friends, or who live in substandard housing) also suffer. Who are we to decide that their suffering shouldn't count? Clearly, advocates argue, these people deserve to be included when we speak of "homelessness."

There are, then, two questions about definitions that ought to be asked whenever we encounter statistics about social problems. First, how is the problem defined? It is all too easy to gloss over definitions, to assume that everybody knows what it means to be homeless or illiterate or whatever. But the specifics of definitions make a difference, and we need to know what they are. Second, is the definition reasonable? No definition is perfect. Definitions that are too narrow exclude false negatives (cases that ought to be included), while definitions that are too broad include false positives (cases that ought to be excluded). It is difficult to have a sensible discussion about a social problem if we can't define the problem in a way that we can agree is reasonable. But even if we cannot agree, we can at least recognize the differences in—and the limitations of—our definitions.

MEASURING

Any statistic based on more than a guess requires some sort of counting. Definitions specify what will be counted. Measuring involves deciding how to go about counting. We cannot begin counting until we decide how we will identify and count instances of a social problem.*

To understand the significance of measurement, let's begin by considering one of the most common ways social scientists measure social concern—survey research. Surveys (or polls) involve asking people questions, counting their answers, and drawing general conclusions based on the results. (Choosing which people to survey presents special problems that we'll consider in the next section, on sampling.) For example, we might ask 1,000 people whether they favor or oppose a new law; if we discover that 500 of the people asked favor the law and 500 oppose it, we might generalize from those findings and conclude that public opinion is about evenly split.

Although the media sometimes report survey results as though public issues involve clear-cut splits in opinions—implying that people either favor or oppose gun control, that they're either pro-choice or pro-life—this is an oversimplification. *Public attitudes toward most social issues are too complex to be*

*In fact, researchers recognize that what I'm calling measurement actually is a type of definition. They refer to *operational definitions,* that is, the operations one goes through to identify an instance of whatever is being defined.

classified in simple pros and cons, or to be measured by a single survey question. For example, surveys find that about 90 percent of Americans agree that legal abortions should be available to women whose health would be endangered by continuing their pregnancies (see Table 1). Pro-choice advocates sometimes interpret such results as evidence that most Americans support legalized abortion. However, surveys also find that only about 45 percent of Americans support abortion regardless of the woman's reason for wanting it, and pro-life advocates sometimes view this as evidence that most Americans oppose abortion on demand. Combining the responses to these questions (as well as others measuring attitudes toward abortion under various circumstances) reveals a more complex pattern of public opinion: there is a small, hard-core antiabortion faction (roughly 10 percent of the population) that opposes abortion under any circumstances; a larger minority (roughly 45 percent) that accepts women's right to choose abortion under almost any circumstances; and another large minority (roughly 45 percent) that occupies a territory between these extremes, that approves of abortion for "good" reasons but does not approve of all abortions, regardless of the circumstances. Attitudes toward abortion are too complicated to be measured by a single survey question or to be described in terms of simple pro/con categories. Obviously, then, measurement makes a difference. The choice of questions used to measure abortion attitudes affects what public opinion surveys discover.

Survey researchers know that *how questions are worded affects results.* Advocates who can afford to sponsor their own surveys

Table 1. *Percentages of Americans Favoring Legal Abortions under Different Circumstances, 1996*

If the woman's own health is seriously endangered by the pregnancy	92
If she became pregnant as a result of rape	84
If there is a strong chance of serious defect in the baby	82
If she is married and does not want any more children	47
If the family has a very low income and cannot afford any more children	47
If she is not married and does not want to marry the man	45
If the woman wants it for any reason	45

SOURCE: Data from the 1996 General Social Survey, from "The American Survey—Release 1997" (CD-ROM; Bellevue, Wash.: Micro-Case, 1997).

can shape the results; usually they try to demonstrate widespread public support for their position. (This is sometimes called *advocacy research.*) Advocates word questions so as to encourage people to respond in the desired way. For example, surveys by gun-control advocates may ask: "Do you favor cracking down against illegal gun sales?" Most people can be counted on to oppose illegal acts, and such questions routinely find that (according to the gun-control activists' interpretations of the results) more than three-quarters of Americans favor gun control. On the other hand, the National Rifle Association opposes gun control, and it sponsors surveys that word questions very differently, such as: "Would you favor or oppose a law giving police the power to decide who may or may not own a firearm?" Not unexpectedly, most people answer that they oppose giving the police so much power, and the NRA can report that most Americans (roughly three-quarters) oppose gun control.[21] As in the example of abortion discussed above, public opinion seems to divide into minorities at the two extremes (some favoring a ban on all guns; others opposed to any gun control), and a large middle mass that, presumably, favors keeping guns out of the hands of "bad" people while letting "good" people have guns. However, the complexity of public opinion can be hard to recognize when our information comes from surveys sponsored by advocates who word questions to produce the results they desire.*

In addition to wording questions to encourage some responses, *advocates who conduct their own surveys can decide how to interpret the results.* A few years ago, the press reported that a national survey estimated that 2 percent of adult Americans (nearly four million people) had been abducted by UFOs. How did the researchers arrive at this figure? Did they ask: "Have you ever been abducted by a UFO?" No. The researchers argued that such a straightforward question would be a poor measure because many UFO abductees do not realize they've been abducted (or are unwilling to talk about the experience);

---

*Although I have chosen to focus on question wording, there are many other ways researchers can design surveys to encourage particular responses. For example, the order in which questions are asked can make a difference in how people respond.

therefore they could not (or would not) answer a direct question accurately. (Note that this is another instance of advocates trying to avoid false negatives; in this case, they did not want to measure abduction in a way that might exclude some cases they felt ought to be included.) Instead, the researchers devised a very different measure: they identified five indicators or symptoms that often figured in the accounts of people who say they've been abducted, and then asked whether respondents had experienced these more innocuous symptoms, for example: "Waking up paralyzed with a sense of a strange person or presence or something else in the room?" They then concluded that anyone who reported four or more symptoms probably had been abducted. Two percent of the survey respondents fell into this group, leading to the researchers' conclusion that 2 percent of the population had been abducted.[22]

This example illustrates the importance of measurement decisions. Measurement involves choices. Had the UFO researchers decided that only one or two symptoms indicated abduction, they would have found more abductees. Had they decided to insist that respondents report all five symptoms, they would have found fewer. (And, of course, had they decided to only count people who reported having been abducted, they presumably would have found fewer yet.) Such choices shape the results of many surveys. Based on affirmative answers to such questions as "Have you had sexual intercourse when you didn't want to because a man gave you alcohol or drugs?" one survey concluded that roughly a quarter of female college students had been raped.[23] Critics challenged this finding; they argued that the questions were ambiguous, and noted that nearly three-quarters of the respondents identified as rape victims indicated they did not consider the incident a rape.[24] But, as these examples demonstrate, it is the advocates conducting the surveys—not the respondents—who create the measurements and interpret the results, who identify the victims of UFO abduction or rape.

Activists justify such measurement decisions as efforts to reveal the true scope of social problems. Remember that activists usually believe that the problem they seek to bring to public attention is both large and largely unrecognized, that there is a substantial dark figure of hidden cases. They design their research to shed light into this darkness; they try to collect data that will reveal the true (substantial) extent of the problem. Therefore, *they devise measurements that will minimize false negatives.* Survey researchers know many techniques for encouraging respondents to give the desired answers. In addition to wording questions carefully, for example, one researcher advises that surveys can elicit more reports of violence against women by: defining violence broadly; asking women about violent incidents throughout their lives (rather than focusing on only, say, the previous year); asking multiple questions about victimization (rather than having a single question); asking open-ended questions that invite wide-ranging responses; and employing sympathetic female interviewers.[25] And, of course, the researcher has the ultimate power to decide which responses indicate the presence of the social problem.

Often, *measurement decisions are hidden.* The media report

statistics ("Research shows that . . .") without explaining how the study measured the social problem. These reports usually ignore controversies about measurement, and even well-established measures can be controversial. For example, the U.S. Bureau of the Census calculates the poverty line—the income levels below which people are considered poor. First established in 1964, the poverty line involves a set of calculations: first, the government determined a food budget for a nutritionally sound diet for a family of four; then, assuming that families spend one-third of their income on food, the bureau multiplied that figure by three. This produced the total income for the base poverty line (which was adjusted for families of different sizes). Each year, the poverty line is multiplied by the change in the Consumer Price Index to take inflation into account. Obviously, the poverty line is an arbitrary standard; different assumptions could be used to justify setting the line higher or lower. In fact, every element in the current formula has come under attack. Critics have argued that the food budget is unrealistic, that the poor do not spend one-third of their income on food, that the Consumer Price Index does not accurately measure inflation, that maintaining the same formula for calculating the poverty line fails to take changes in the standard of living into account, and so on.[26] There is, for instance, a debate over what ought to count as family income: if a family gets food stamps, should the value of its food stamps be considered income? Imagine a family that earns an income just below the poverty line; if the value of the food stamps it receives plus its income produces a total above the line, should it still be considered poor?

How to measure poverty has been a contentious issue for decades. In general, political liberals favor measurement choices that raise the poverty line or make it harder to meet the threshold; they oppose, for example, treating the value of food stamps as income. Measuring poverty in this way means that more people will be considered poor (and therefore deserving additional social services). In contrast, most conservatives argue that the poverty line ought to be set low and that it should be easy to exceed; thus, they favor counting food stamps as income. Such measurement choices will identify fewer poor people (therefore supporting arguments that there is less need for social services). In this debate, liberals argue that the established poverty line produces too many false negatives (that is, too many people who are "really" poor fall above the line), while conservatives charge that the poverty line designates false positives (too many people who "really" aren't poor fall below the line).

Like definitions, measurements always involve choices. Advocates of different measures can defend their own choices and criticize those made by their opponents—so long as the various choices being made are known and understood. However, when measurement choices are kept hidden, it becomes difficult to assess the statistics based on those choices.

SAMPLING

Virtually all social statistics involve generalizing from samples. It is usually too difficult and too expensive to count every instance of some social condition; it is cheaper, faster, and more efficient to select some cases, examine them, and then generalize to the larger social problem. In the specialized vocabulary of statisticians, the cases examined are a *sample* chosen to represent the larger *population* of all cases.

There are two problems with sampling—one obvious, and the other more subtle. The obvious problem is sample size. Samples tend to be much smaller than their populations. Even national surveys (such as the Gallup Poll) usually interview only 1,000 to 2,000 people. Many studies by social scientists use much smaller samples; it is not uncommon for social research to be based on interviews with only a few dozen people. Obviously, it is possible to question results based on small samples. The smaller the sample, the less confidence we have that the sample accurately reflects the population.

However, large samples aren't necessarily good samples. This leads to the second issue: *the representativeness of a sample is actually far more important than sample size.* A good sample accurately reflects (or "represents") the population. If tens of thousands of readers fill out a questionnaire they find in a magazine and mail in their responses, it is not at all clear what population they represent. Some kinds of people will be much more likely to read the magazine than others, and readers who complete the questionnaire will differ from those who don't; the resulting sample—however large—is not representative.

Selecting a representative sample is a key challenge in social science. Ideally, researchers know the full extent of the population they want to study, and they can select a sample from this population at random. Statisticians can calculate the probability that such *random samples* represent the population; this is usually expressed in terms of *sampling error* (for example, there might be a 95 percent probability that the distribution of responses in a sample will be within 3 percent of the distribution in the population).

The real problem is that few samples are random. Even when researchers know the nature of the population, it can be time-consuming and expensive to draw a random sample; all too often, it is impossible to draw a true random sample because the population cannot be defined. This is particularly true for studies of social problems. Because social problems always have hidden cases (the dark figure), the actual dimensions of the population always are uncertain. Suppose we want to study teenage runaways. How can we identify the runaway population (which, after all, changes from minute to minute as some teenagers run away and others return home)? Some runaways are gone for minutes or a few hours; other leave for years, even permanently. Some go to stay with friends or relatives; others live on the streets. With such a fluid, diverse population, drawing a random sample presents terrible challenges. Researchers have to make compromises, to draw the best samples they can; they might, for example, combine different samples—perhaps randomly sampling shelters to identify long-term runaways *and* sampling teenagers drawn from the general population to try and identify some former short-term runaways who have returned home. The best samples are those that come as close as possible to being random.

But *statistics about social problems usually are based on samples that fall far short of randomness.* People who want to promote new social problems may not think critically about the representativeness of the samples that serve as the basis for their statistics. Remember that activists tend to spend their time among people intensely concerned about their social problem; they share stories about the severity of the problem and generally reaffirm one another's concern. They probably feel that this experience gives them a pretty good sense of the nature of the problem, and that the cases they encounter are fairly typical. Thus, someone who works in a particular runaway shelter and sees the teenagers who come there may decide to collect statistics on the shelter's clients. The great advantage of this method is its convenience—the runaways come to you. This is called *convenience sampling;* it is inexpensive, it is easy, and it is by far the most common way to study social problems.

The disadvantage with convenience samples, of course, is that it is hard to know whether they reflect the population. Suppose we keep track of all the runaways who pass through one shelter in a month. What population do they represent? Certainly we cannot argue that they represent all runaways, because many runaways never go near a shelter. Well, do they at least represent the population of all runaways who visit shelters? Maybe—but maybe not: there may well be differences in the runaways who come to different shelters, depending on the region where the city is located (warm versus cold climate), shelter policies (shelters may have different rules for admitting runaways), whether a city's runaways have a choice of places they can go to get help, and so on. An apparently conservative answer might be that our sample at least represents the population of runaways who pass through that shelter. But does it? It might depend on which month we decided to collect data: there are probably more runaways in summer months (because it is warm and school is out); winter runaways might be different (more committed, or more desperate). The potential limitations of convenience samples always need to be considered.

A related problem emerges when activists select particular cases to illustrate a social problem. Recall that activists often choose vivid examples to raise concern; they pick these cases precisely because they are not typical, but are especially dramatic and arouse our shock, horror, anger, or outrage. There is, of course, nothing random about the choice of these examples. However, advocates may talk about these cases as though they are somehow typical, representative of the larger problem. A murdered runaway is a tragic story that may capture media attention and mobilize public concern, but the case is a poor basis for generalizing to the larger problem of teenage runaways. Terrible examples should not be treated as though they are representative samples of a social problem.

The difficulties of drawing accurate samples also invite another sort of generalizing claim. Activists sometimes take advantage of a social problem's dark figure to speculate about the problem's scope. For example, they may argue that the problem threatens "everyone," that it affects "people of all sorts," even that it strikes "at random." Thus, an advocate might argue that teenagers run away from all sorts of families, that it is impossible to predict which teenagers might become runaways. Such claims are powerful because they raise everyone's concern: if any teenager might run away, then runaways could happen in families you know; even someone in your family might run away. But there is a difference between saying that some teenagers run away from upper-middle-class families that have both parents present ("It happens!") and saying that teenagers from such families are just as likely to run away as other teenagers. All teenagers may be at *some* risk of running away, but that does not mean that all teenagers have the *same* risk of becoming runaways. In general, social problems are *patterned;* people do not run away—or commit crimes, become homeless, or become infected with HIV—at random. But *people promoting social problems often find it advantageous to gloss over these patterns,* to imply that everyone shares the same risks and therefore we all have the same, substantial stake in solving the social problem.[27]

In short, the process of generalization is at the center of sampling. People who talk about social problems almost inevitably want to generalize from some cases—a sample—to the larger problem. The key question is what sorts of generalizations the sample permits. Researchers able to draw random samples from populations that are well understood can make convincing generalizations. But this is almost never possible in analyses of social problems, especially when the problem is first coming to public attention. At that early stage, the dark figure is usually unknown, but probably large, and advocates often don't even have a clear sense of what they don't know. They generalize on the basis of the minimal evidence they do have: perhaps they know about some dramatic examples that might serve to arouse public concern; perhaps they have conducted studies based on convenience samples of cases that have come to their attention; perhaps they believe that the largely hidden problem is so widespread that it reaches every corner of society. Their limited knowledge, coupled with their enthusiasm for the cause, encourages them to make generalizations that cannot be supported by the evidence.

The media often fail to question activists' generalizations. Frightening examples and claims that a problem threatens everyone make good, compelling news stories. And, if reporters do try to check the activists' generalizations, they may be unable to find anyone with better evidence. Only later, after the problem is defined as a matter of serious public concern, are experts likely to design careful, authoritative research projects. Such research can be expensive, particularly when it tries to examine a random—or at least, an approximately random—sample of a reasonable size. Usually, careful research of this sort requires funding from major institutions—government agencies, foundations, or industries—and they are unlikely to sponsor such work until activists have convinced them to make the problem a priority.

Again, virtually all claims about social problems involve generalizing from a sample of cases. We need to ask how much confidence we should have in these generalizations, and the answer to this question will depend on the nature and quality of the sample. Advocates ought to clearly explain the nature of their sample, so that others can evaluate the strength of the generalizations the sample will support.

CHARACTERISTICS OF GOOD STATISTICS

This chapter's focus has been the production of bad statistics through guessing, dubious definitions, questionable measurement, and poor sampling. At this point, you may be wondering whether all statistics are bad, nothing more than "damned lies." Are there any good statistics? How can we tell the good numbers from the bad?

The problems identified in this chapter suggest some standards that good statistics meet. First, *good statistics are based on more than guessing*. The most basic question about any statistic is: How did someone arrive at this number? All statistics are imperfect, but some flaws are worse than others. Obviously, we should not place too much confidence in guesses (even educated guesses). Watch for the danger signs of guessing: Do the people offering the statistic have a bias—do they want to show that the problem is common (or rare)? Is the statistic a big, round number? Does the statistic describe an unfamiliar, hidden social problem that probably has a large dark figure (if so, how did the advocates manage to come up with their numbers)?

Second, *good statistics are based on clear, reasonable definitions*. Remember, every statistic has to define its subject. Those definitions ought to be clear and made public. An example—particularly a dramatic, disturbing example, a horror story, a worst case—is not a definition. Anyone presenting a statistic describing a social problem should be able and willing to explain the definition used to create the statistic. Definitions usually are broad: they encompass kinds of cases very different from (and usually less serious than) the examples. We need to ask: How broad? What does the definition include? Again, ask yourself whether the people offering the statistic favor broad (or narrow) definitions, and why. Consider whether their definition might exclude too many false negatives or include too many false positives.

Third, *good statistics are based on clear, reasonable measures.* Again, every statistic involves some sort of measurement; while all measures are imperfect, not all flaws are equally serious. People offering a statistic should be able and willing to explain how they measured the social problem, and their choices should seem reasonable. If the people offering the statistic have some sort of bias (in favor of big—or small—numbers), that bias may be reflected in the way they've measured the problem. For example, they may have worded survey questions to encourage certain responses, or they may interpret responses in peculiar ways. Be suspicious of statistics based on hidden measurements, and consider how measurement choices might shape statistics.

Finally, *good statistics are based on good samples.* Clear, reasonable definitions and clear, reasonable measurements are not enough. Almost all statistics generalize from a sample of cases to a larger population, and the methods of selecting that sample should be explained. Good samples are representative of that larger population; ideally, this means the sample has been selected at random. Watch out for statistics based on small, nonrandom, convenience samples; such samples are easier and cheaper to study, but they are a poor basis for sweeping generalizations. Ask yourself how the sample chosen might skew the resulting statistics.

One sign of good statistics is that we're given more than a number; we're told something about the definitions, measurement, and sampling behind the figure—about how the number emerged. When that information remains concealed, we have every reason to be skeptical.

3

MUTANT STATISTICS

Methods for Mangling Numbers

Not all statistics start out bad, but any statistic can be made worse. Numbers—even good numbers—can be misunderstood or misinterpreted. Their meanings can be stretched, twisted, distorted, or mangled. These alterations create what we can call *mutant statistics*—distorted versions of the original figures.

Many mutant statistics have their roots in innumeracy. Remember that innumeracy—difficulties grasping the meanings of numbers and calculations—is widespread. The general public may be innumerate, but often the advocates promoting social problems are not any better. They may become confused about a number's precise meaning; they may misunderstand how the problem has been defined, how it has been measured, or what sort of sampling has been used. At the same time, their commitment to their cause and their enthusiasm for promoting the problem ("After all, it's a big problem!") may lead them to "improve" the statistic, to make the numbers seem more dramatic, even more compelling. Some mutant statistics may be products of advocates' cynicism, of their deliberate attempts to distort information in order to make their claims more convincing; this seems particularly likely when mutation occurs at the hands of large institutions that twist information into the form most favorable to their vested interests. But mutation can also be a product of sincere, albeit muddled interpretations by innumerate advocates.

Once someone utters a mutant statistic, there is a good chance that those who hear it will accept it and repeat it. Innumerate advocates influence their audiences: the media repeat mutant statistics; and the public accepts—or at least does not challenge—whatever numbers the media present. A political leader or a respected commentator may hear a statistic and repeat it, making the number seem even more credible. As statistics gain wide circulation, number laundering occurs. The figures become harder to challenge because everyone has heard them, everyone assumes the numbers must be correct. Particularly when numbers reinforce our beliefs, prejudices, or interests ("Of course that's true!"), we take figures as facts, without subjecting them to criticism.

Consider one widely circulated statistic about the dangers of anorexia nervosa (the term for eating dangerously little in an effort to be thin). Anorexia usually occurs in young women, and some feminists argue that it is a response to societal pressures for women to be beautiful, and cultural standards that equate slenderness with beauty. Activists seeking to draw attention to the problem estimated that 150,000 American women were anorexic, and noted that anorexia could lead to death.[1] At some point, feminists began reporting that each year 150,000 women *died* from anorexia.[2] (This was a considerable exaggeration; only about 70 deaths per year are attributed to anorexia.) This simple transformation—turning an estimate for the total number of anorexic women into the annual number of fatalities—produced a dramatic, memorable statistic. Advocates repeated the erroneous figure in influential books, in newspaper columns, on talk shows, and so on. There were soon numerous sources for the mistaken number. A student searching for material for a term paper on anorexia, for instance, had a good chance of encountering—and repeating—this wildly inaccurate statistic, and each repetition helped ensure that the mutant statistic would live on.

Yet it should have been obvious that something was wrong with this figure. Anorexia typically affects *young* women. In the United States each year, roughly 8,500 females aged 15–24 die from all causes; another 47,000 women aged 25–44 also die.[3] What were the chances, then, that there could be 150,000 deaths from anorexia each year? But, of course, most of us have no idea how many young women die each year ("It must be a lot. . . ."). When we hear that anorexia kills 150,000 young women per year, we assume that whoever cites the number must know that it is true. We accept the mutant statistic, and may even repeat it ourselves.

Once created, *mutant statistics have a good chance of spreading and enduring.* But how and why does mutation occur? This chapter explores four common ways of creating mutant num-

MUTANT STATISTICS

bers. It begins with the most basic errors—making inappropriate *generalizations* from a statistic. It then turns to *transformations*—taking a number that means one thing and interpreting it to mean something completely different. The third section concerns *confusion*—transformations that involve misunderstanding the meaning of more complicated statistics. Finally, we'll consider *compound errors*—the ways in which bad statistics can be linked to form chains of error. In these four ways, bad statistics not only take on lives of their own, but they do increasing damage as they persist.

GENERALIZATION: ELEMENTARY FORMS OF ERROR

Generalization is an essential step in statistical reasoning. We rarely are able to count all the cases of some social problem. Instead, we collect some evidence, usually from a sample, and generalize from it to the larger problem. The process of generalization involves the basic processes discussed in chapter 2: the problem must be defined, and a means of measurement and a sample must be chosen. These are elementary steps in social research. The basic principles are known: definitions and measures need to be clear and reasonable; samples should be representative. But even the most basic principles can be violated and, surprisingly often, no one notices when this happens. Mutant statistics—based on flawed definitions, poor measurements, or bad samples—emerge, and often receive a surprising amount of attention.

Questionable Definitions

Consider the flurry of media coverage about an "epidemic" of fires in African American churches in the South in 1996. Various advocates charged that the fires were the work of a racist conspiracy.[4] Their claims recalled the history of racial terrorism in the South; black churches had often been targets of arson or bombing. Perhaps because 1996 was an election year, politicians—both Democrats (including President Clinton and Vice President Gore) and Republicans—denounced the fires, as did both the liberal National Council of Churches and the conservative Christian Coalition. Virtually everyone spoke out against the wave of arson.

Activists (such as the antiracist Center for Democratic Renewal) tried to document the increased number of fires; they produced lists of church arsons and statistics about the number of suspicious fires as evidence that the problem was serious. However, investigations, first by journalists and later by a federal task force, called these claims into question.[5] While there were certainly some instances in which whites burned black churches out of racist motives, there was no evidence that a conspiracy linked the various fires. Moreover, the definition of a suspicious church fire proved to be unclear; the activists' lists included fires at churches with mostly white congregations, fires known to have been set by blacks, or by teenage vandals, or by mentally disturbed individuals, and fires set in order to collect insurance. And, when journalists checked the records of the fire insurance industry, they discovered not only that the number of fires in

1996 was not unusually high, but that church arsons had been generally declining since at least 1980. The federal task force ultimately failed to find any evidence of either an epidemic of fires or a conspiracy, although the press gave the task force report little coverage and advocates denounced the study's findings.

In short, statistics attempting to demonstrate the existence of an epidemic of church arsons lacked a clear definition of what ought to count as a racially motivated church fire. Nor did advocates define how many fires it would take to constitute an "epidemic" (although it would presumably be some number above the normal annual total of church fires). The absence of any clear definitions made it difficult to assess the evidence. The advocates who offered lists of fires (and asserted that each blaze was evidence of a racist conspiracy) may have been convinced, but those who tried to identify cases using some sort of clear definition failed to find any evidence that the epidemic even existed.

Inadequate Measurement

Clear, precise definitions are not enough. Whatever is defined must also be measured, and meaningless measurements will produce meaningless statistics. For instance, consider recent federal efforts to count hate crimes (crimes motivated by racial, religious, or other prejudice).

In response to growing concern about hate crimes, the federal government began collecting hate-crime statistics. The Federal Bureau of Investigation invited local law enforcement agencies to submit annual reports on hate crimes within their jurisdictions and, beginning in 1991, the bureau began issuing national hate-crime statistics.

Although the FBI had collected data on the incidence of crime from local agencies for decades, counting hate crimes posed special problems.[6] When police record a reported crime—say, a robbery—it is a relatively straightforward process: usually the victim comes forward and tells of being forced to surrender money to the robber; these facts let the police classify the crime as a robbery. But identifying a hate crime requires something more: an assessment of the criminal's *motive*. A robbery might be a hate crime—*if* prejudice motivates the robber—but the crimes committed by robbers with other motives are not hate crimes. There are real disagreements about how to define and measure hate crimes. Not surprisingly, some activists favor broad, inclusive standards that will avoid false negatives; some feminists, for example, argue that rapes automatically should be considered hate crimes (on the grounds that all rape is motivated by gender prejudice).[7] But local officials (who may be reluctant to publicize tensions within their communities) may favor much narrower standards, so that a cross-burning on an African American family's lawn may be classified as a "teenage prank," rather than a hate crime, depending on how police assess the offenders' motives.[8]

Because there is much variation in how—and even whether—agencies measure hate crimes, hate-crime statistics have been incomplete and uneven. In 1991, the FBI collected hate-crime data from agencies in only 32 states; less than a quarter of all law enforcement agencies supplied reports. By 1996, 49 states and the

District of Columbia reported some data, but many agencies still did not participate. More important, many of the agencies that did file reports indicated that they had recorded no hate crimes during 1996: 12 states reported fewer than 10 hate crimes apiece; Alabama's law enforcement agencies did not report a single hate crime.[9] So long as many agencies refused to submit hate-crime statistics—and others used wildly different standards to classify hate crimes—the data collected and published would have little value. We might even suspect that the jurisdictions that report the most hate crimes will be those with the most liberal governments, because they are more likely to press law enforcement agencies to take reporting seriously. This suggests that hate-crime statistics may be a better measure of local officials' politics than of the incidence of hate crimes.

While the recordkeeping may improve over time, the hate-crime statistics reported during the program's early years were nearly worthless. The organizational practices for recording hate crimes obviously varied widely among jurisdictions, making meaningful comparisons impossible. Moreover, it should be noted that, as reporting does improve, the numbers of reported hate crimes will almost certainly increase. That is, incidents that previously would not have been counted as hate crimes will be counted, and successive annual reports will show the incidence of hate crime rising. It may be years before measurement becomes sufficiently standardized to permit meaningful comparisons among jurisdictions, or from year to year. Measurement is always important, but this example illustrates why new statistical measures should be handled with special caution.

Bad Samples

Chapter 2 emphasized the importance of generalizing from representative samples. This is a basic principle, but one that is easily lost. For example, consider a study subtitled "A Survey of 917,410 Images, Descriptions, Short Stories, and Animations Downloaded 8.5 Million Times by Consumers in Over 2000 Cities in Forty Countries, Provinces, and Territories."[10] An undergraduate student published this research in 1995 in a law review; he reported that 83.5 percent of the downloaded images were pornographic. In 1995, the Internet was still a novel phenomenon; people worried that children were frequent users, and that parents did not understand the Internet well enough to protect their children from questionable content. Claims that an extensive research project revealed that a substantial majority of Internet traffic involved pornography generated considerable concern. The huge scope of the study—917,410 images downloaded 8.5 million times—implied that it must be exhaustive.

But, of course, a large sample is not necessarily a good sample. In this case, the researcher did not collect a representative sample of Internet traffic. Rather, he examined postings to only 17 of some 32 Usenet groups that carried image files. Phrased differently, his findings showed that pornographic images accounted for only about 3 percent of Usenet traffic, while Usenet accounted for only about an eighth of the traffic on the entire Internet.[11] In short, the sample of images was drawn from precisely that portion of the Internet where pornographic images were concentrated; it was anything but a representative sample.

An alternative way to summarize the study's findings was that only 0.5 percent of Internet traffic involved pornographic images—a markedly lower (and less dramatic) figure than 83.5 percent. This example reminds us that mistaking a large sample for a representative sample can be a serious error.

The three cases discussed in this section—the unfocused definition of church fires, the uneven measurement of hate crimes, and the biased sample of Internet traffic—reveal that the most basic flaws can distort statistics about social problems. All three of these cases received extensive coverage from the media; all three attracted concerned attention from political leaders; and all three cases involved mutant statistics. It is also true that, in all three cases, those statistics eventually drew criticism. However, critics are not always successful in influencing the public. Many people probably remain convinced that most Internet traffic is pornographic, that members of a racist conspiracy set many church fires, and so on. Mutant statistics often prove to be long-lived.

TRANSFORMATION:
CHANGING THE MEANING OF STATISTICS

Another common form of mutant statistic involves transforming a number's meaning. Usually, this involves someone who tries to repeat a number, but manages to say something different. This chapter's introduction offers an example: recall that 150,000 *people with* anorexia became 150,000 *deaths from* anorexia. Of course, not all transformations are as obvious as equating having a disease with dying from it. Often transformations involve more subtle misunderstandings or logical leaps.

Consider the evolution of one critic's estimate that "six percent of America's 52,000 [Roman Catholic] priests are at some point in their adult lives sexually preoccupied with minors."[12] This estimate originated with a psychologist and former priest who treated disturbed clergy and derived the figure from his observations. It was, in short, an educated guess. Still, his claim was often repeated (it was undoubtedly the only statistic available) and, in the process, transformed in at least four important ways.[13] First, some of those who repeated the figure forgot that it was an estimate, and referred to the number as though it were a well-established fact—presumably a finding from a survey of priests. Second, while the psychologist's estimate was based on a sample of priests who had sought psychological treatment (and therefore might well be especially likely to have experienced inappropriate attractions to young people), he generalized to all priests. Third, although the original estimate referred to sexual *attraction*, rather than actual behavior, those who repeated the number often suggested that 6 percent of all priests had had sexual contacts with young people. Fourth, those young people became redefined as "children"; critics charged that 6 percent of priests were pedophiles ("pedophiles" are adults who have sex with prepubescent children). Although the original estimate in fact suggested that twice as many priests were attracted to adolescents as to younger children, this subtlety was lost. Thus, an estimate that perhaps 6 percent of priests in treatment were at some point sexually attracted to young people was transformed into the fact that 6 percent of all priests had had sex with children. Not everyone who repeated the statistic made all four transformations, but the number's original meaning soon became lost in a chorus of claims linking "pedophile priests" to the 6 percent figure.

This example suggests that a single statistic can be transformed in several ways, that it is impossible to predict all the ways a number might be misunderstood and given an entirely new meaning. While it may be especially easy to transform estimates and guesses (because the language of guessing is often vague), even more precisely defined statistics can undergo transformation.

Homicide statistics offer an example. In addition to gathering reports of homicides in order to calculate crime rates, the FBI also tries to collect more detailed information for its Supplementary Homicide Reports (SHR). The FBI encourages law enforcement agencies to complete a brief SHR form for each homicide; the form asks, for example, about the victim's age, gender, and ethnicity, the relationship between victim and offender, and the circumstances of the homicide (for example, whether the death occurred during the course of a robbery, during an argument, and so on).

SHR data are inevitably incomplete. When the police find the body of a homicide victim, they may not know enough to complete the entire SHR form: they ordinarily can identify the victim's age and gender, and they often—but not always—can specify the circumstances of the homicide, but unless they identify the offender, they usually cannot know the nature of the victim-offender relationship. In such cases, the relationship is coded "unknown." Roughly 15 to 20 percent of SHR reports list the circumstances as unknown; nearly 40 percent indicate that the victim-offender relationship is unknown.[14]

It is important to realize that completing the SHR paperwork is a by-product of police work and may receive a relatively low priority in many departments. Agencies are supposed to submit SHR reports within five days of the end of the month when the homicide becomes known. While the FBI asks for updated reports when additional information becomes available, many agencies do not bother to report changes. Thus, a homicide initially reported as involving unknown circumstances or an unknown victim-offender relationship may later be solved, but the police do not necessarily report what more they have learned to the FBI.

An SHR classification of "unknown" means just that—at the time the report was completed, the police didn't have some information. However, people sometimes make assumptions about the nature of the unknown circumstances or unknown victim-offender relationships reported to the FBI. In the early 1980s, the FBI drew attention to the problem of serial murder (that is, individuals who killed victims on more than one occasion).[15] There had been several prominent serial murder cases in the news, and the press argued that this was, if not a new crime problem, at least one that was more common than ever before. The FBI estimated that there might be as many as 35 serial murderers active at any one time, and the media claimed that serial murderers might account for as many as 4,000 or 5,000 deaths per year. (Some commentators mangled these numbers further, reporting that there were 4–5,000 active serial killers.) It should have been apparent that there was something wrong with these statistics: they implied that each killer murdered more than 100 victims per year—an improbably high average. How did the advocates arrive at the figure of 4,000 victims? Simple: they assumed that all—or at least a large share—of SHR homicides involving unknown circumstances or an unknown victim-offender relationship were serial murders. Serial murderers often kill victims unknown to them; therefore, the advocates assumed, cases in which the victim-offender relationship was unknown were probably serial murder cases.

Recent claims blaming most homicides on strangers use similar logic. SHR reports classify about 15 percent of victims and offenders as strangers, but nearly 40 percent of victim-offender relationships as unknown. Some interpretations assumed that any unknown relationship must involve strangers; they added 15 percent and 40 percent and concluded that strangers commit most (55 percent) murders.[16]

Both the serial murder and the stranger-homicide claims transformed the meaning of "unknown" by assuming that, if the police can't classify the victim-offender relationship, then the homicide must be the work of a stranger—or even a serial killer. This is an unwarranted logical leap. Researchers who have conducted more careful and more complete studies (for example, examining officials' final classifications for homicides) have concluded that strangers account for 20–25 percent of all homicides (not more than half), and that serial murderers kill perhaps 400 victims per year (not 4,000).

The lesson from the misinterpretation of SHR statistics, then, concerns transformations created by careless inferences about the meaning of official statistics. In these cases, advocates assumed that they knew what had actually happened in cases that the police labeled "unknown." They produced dramatic, frightening figures that exaggerated the deaths caused by strangers or serial murderers, and those transformed figures received wide circulation.

Transformations involve shifts in meaning; advocates convert a statistic about X into a statistic about Y. This is an obvious error. Sometimes transformations are inadvertent; they reflect nothing more than sloppy, imprecise language. In such cases, people try to repeat a statistic, but they accidentally reword a claim in a way that creates a whole new meaning. Of course, other transformations may be deliberate efforts to mislead in order to advance the advocates' cause.

Certainly *transformations often "improve" a claim by making it more dramatic:* the number of anorexics becomes a body count; priests attracted to adolescents become priests having sex with children; homicides of unknown circumstances become serial killings. Such statistics get repeated precisely because they are dramatic, compelling numbers. A transformation that makes a statistic seem less dramatic is likely to be forgotten, but a more dramatic number stands a good chance of being repeated. It is a statistical version of Gresham's Law: *bad statistics drive out good ones.*

And there is another lesson: transformation errors often reflect innumeracy. Both advocates and their audiences fail to think critically about the numbers being circulated. It should have been obvious that anorexia could not kill 150,000 women per year. Similarly, the people who asserted that there were 35 active serial murderers killing 4,000 victims each year should have realized that those two figures made no sense when combined, that both could not be correct.

Obviously, advocates who make transformations reveal their innumeracy, but advocates are not the only ones to blame. The media and the others who repeat the claims also make blunders. The reporters who wrote stories about all those deaths from anorexia or serial murder should have asked themselves whether those numbers were plausible; they might even have investigated the claims before repeating them. Yet, in each case, these numbers received wide circulation for years—and continued to be repeated even after they were called into question. After all, the mutant statistics were now readily available; people easily could find them on the Internet or printed in many sources. *Transformation errors are easy to make, but difficult to set right.*

Transformation only requires that one person misunderstand a statistic and repeat the number in a way that gives it a new meaning. Once that new meaning—the mutant statistic—is available, many of the ways people may respond to it—accepting it, repeating it, or simply not challenging it—help maintain the error. Even if someone recognizes the mistake and calls attention to it, the error is likely to live on, uncorrected in many people's minds.

CONFUSION: GARBLING COMPLEX STATISTICS

The examples we've discussed so far in this chapter involve mis-understanding relatively simple, straightforward statistics. But some statistics get mangled because they seem too difficult to grasp, and therefore they are easily confused. (Be warned: the examples that follow are more complicated than those in the other sections of this chapter. While you will not need any sophisticated mathematical knowledge in order to make sense of the confusion, you must pay attention to the steps by which the statistics were first calculated and then garbled.)

Consider *Workforce 2000*, a 1987 report, commissioned by the U.S. Department of Labor, that projected changes in the American workforce.[17] The population in the workforce is gradually changing for several reasons: most important, a growing proportion of women work, so females account for a growing percentage of workers; in addition, the percentage of workers who are nonwhites is growing (this reflects several developments, including immigration patterns and ethnic differences in birth rates). The combined effect of these changes is gradually to reduce the proportion of white males in the workforce: in 1988 (roughly when *Workforce 2000* appeared), white males accounted for 47.9 percent of all workers; and the report projected that, by 2000, this percentage would fall to 44.8 percent.

However, rather than describing the change in such easily understood terms, the authors of *Workforce 2000* chose to speak of "net additions to the workforce" (see Table 2). What did this term mean? Very simply, the report made predictions about the

Table 2. *Projected Net Additions to the Workforce
by Ethnicity and Sex, 1988–2000*

Worker Category	Projected Net Additions[a]	Percentage
Non-Hispanic white males	2,265,000	11.6
Non-Hispanic white females	6,939,000	35.6
Hispanic males	2,877,000	14.8
Hispanic females	2,464,000	12.7
Black males	1,302,000	6.7
Black females	1,754,000	9.0
Asian & other males	950,000	4.9
Asian & other females	910,000	4.7
Total	19,461,000	100.0

NOTE: The data used in this table are similar to, but not precisely the same as those used to prepare *Workforce 2000*. Therefore, some of the figures are close to—but not precisely the same as—those quoted from the report.

[a] Projected net additions is a total—the number of workers expected to enter the workforce, minus the number expected to leave through death, retirement, and so on.

SOURCE: Howard N. Fullerton, "New Labor Force Projections, Spanning 1988 to 2000," *Monthly Labor Review* 112 (November 1989): 3–11 (Table 7).

populations of workers that would enter and leave the workforce (because of death, retirement, and so on) between 1988 and 2000. For example, the authors estimated that 13.5 million white males would join the workforce and 11.3 million would leave during those years. The difference—2.2 million—would be white males' "net addition to the workforce." Because the numbers of female and nonwhite workers are growing faster than those of white males, white males made up a relatively small share—less than 15 percent—of the anticipated total net addition to the workforce.

Rather than describing the gradual decline in white males' proportion of the workforce in terms of a straightforward percentage (47.9 percent in 1988, falling to 44.8 percent in 2000), the authors of *Workforce 2000* chose to use a more obscure measure (net additions to the workforce). That was an unfortunate choice, because it invited confusion. In fact, it even confused the people who prepared the report. *Workforce 2000* came with an "executive summary"—a brief introduction summarizing the report's key points for those too busy to read the entire document. The *Executive Summary to Workforce 2000* mangled the report's findings by claiming: "Only 15 percent of the new entrants to the labor force over the next 13 years will be native white males, compared to 47 percent in that category today."[18] That sentence was wrong for two reasons: first, it confused *net additions* to the labor force (expected to be roughly 15 percent white males) with all *new entrants* to the labor force (white males were expected to be about 32 percent of all those entering the labor force); and, second, it made a meaningless comparison between the percentage of white males among net workforce entrants and white males' percentage in the existing labor force (roughly 47 percent). The statistical comparison seemed dramatic, but it was pointless.

Unfortunately, the dramatic number captured people's attention. The press fixed on the decline in white male workers as the report's major finding, and they began to repeat the error. Officials at the Department of Labor tried to clarify the confusion, but the mutant statistic predictably took on a life of its own.[19] Politicians, labor and business leaders, and activists all warned that the workplace was about to undergo a sudden change, that white males—historically the typical, the most common category of workers—were an endangered species. The mangled statistic was itself remangled; for example, one official testified before Congress: "By the year 2000, nearly 65% of the total workforce will be women," yet no one asked how or why that might occur.[20] Claims about the vanishing white male worker flourished.

It is easy to see why people repeated these claims; the notion that white males would soon become a small proportion of all workers offered support for very different political ideologies. Liberals saw the coming change as proof that more needed to be done to help women and minorities—who, after all, would be the workers of the future. Liberal proposals based on *Workforce 2000* called for expanded job training for nontraditional (that is, nonwhite or female) workers, additional programs to educate management and workers about the need for diversity in the workplace, and so on. In contrast, conservatives viewed the changing workforce as further evidence that immigration, feminism, and other developments threatened traditional social arrangements. In response to claims that white male workers were disappearing, a wide range of people found it easier to agree ("We knew it! We told you so!") than to ask critical questions about the statistical claims.

The reaction to *Workforce 2000* teaches a disturbing lesson: *complex statistics are prime candidates for mutation*. Not that the statistics in *Workforce 2000* were all that complex—they weren't. But the meaning of "net additions to the workforce" was not obvious, and when people tried to put it in simpler language— such as "new workers"—they mangled the concept. The report's authors made a poor choice when they chose to highlight statistics about net additions; they invited the confusion that followed. They ought to have realized that most people would not grasp this relatively complicated idea. (*Never overestimate the understanding of an innumerate public.*) And, of course, the people who interpreted the report (beginning with the authors of the executive summary!), instead of repeating the statistic, unintentionally mangled it to produce figures with new, wildly distorted meanings. Thus, a correct-but-difficult-to-understand statistic became an easy-to-understand-but-completely-wrong number.

Similar confusion characterized press coverage of a medical study that supposedly showed that physicians referred blacks and women for cardiac catheterization less often than whites and males.[21] In the study, researchers gave doctors information (e.g., descriptions of chest pain and results of stress tests) about fictional patients who were described as either black or white, female or male. The doctors were asked how they would treat these patients, and the researchers examined which kinds of patients were referred for cardiac catheterization. Interestingly, white females, black males, and white males were equally likely to receive referrals for the procedure: catheterization was recommended for 90.6 percent of the patients in each group (see the first column in Table 3). In contrast, only 78.8 percent of black women were referred for catheterization. This study attracted considerable press coverage when the media summarized the results as showing that blacks and women were "40 percent less likely" to receive cardiac testing. How could the press produce this mangled statistic from these data?

The answer lies in the researchers' decision to report their results in terms of *odds ratios*. Producing this statistic involved a two-stage calculation. First, the researchers calculated the odds of people in different groups being referred for catheterization (see the second column in Table 3). Remember that 90.6 percent of white women received referrals; this means that, among 1,000 white women, 906 would get referrals, and 94 would not; therefore the *odds* of a white woman being referred were 9.6 to 1 (906 referrals/94 nonreferrals = 9.6). That is, for every white woman not referred, 9.6 would be referred—this is their odds of referral. Black and white males had the exactly same percentages of being referred, and therefore the same odds of referral, but the odds of black women being referred were only 3.7 to 1 (among 1,000 black women, there would be 788 referrals/212 nonreferrals = 3.7—for every black woman not referred, 3.7 would be referred). Notice (see the lower half of Table 3) that when white males and females are grouped together, because both sexes had the same rates of

Table 3. *Percentage Referred for Cardiac Catheterization,*
Odds of Referral, Odds Ratio, and Risk Ratio, by Sex and Ethnicity

	Mean Referral Rate[a]	Odds of Referral[b]	Odds Ratio[c]	Risk Ratio[d]
Patients				
White men	90.6	9.6 to 1	1.0	
Black men	90.6	9.6 to 1	1.0	
White women	90.6	9.6 to 1	1.0	
Black women	78.8	3.7 to 1	0.4	0.87
Aggregate Data				
All whites	90.6	9.6 to 1	1.0	
All blacks	84.7	5.5 to 1	0.6	0.93
All men	90.6	9.6 to 1	1.0	
All women	84.7	5.5 to 1	0.6	0.93

[a] Percentage of cases in a category referred for catheterization.

[b] The odds of a member of a category being referred = referral rate divided by (100% minus referral rate). For example, 9.6 white males were referred for every white male who was not referred— $90.6/(100-90.6) = 9.6$.

[c] The ratio of the odds of referral for two groups = odds for a group divided by odds for its reference group. For example, odds for black women/odds for white men = $3.7/9.6 = .4$.

[d] The ratio of the referral rates for two groups = referral rate for a group divided by referral rate for its reference group. For example, referral rate for black women/referral rate for white men = $78.8/90.6$ = .87.

SOURCE: Lisa M. Schwartz, Steven Woloshin, and H. Gilbert Welch, "Misunderstandings about the Effects of Race and Sex on Physicians' Referrals for Cardiac Catheterization," *New England Journal of Medicine* 341 (1999): 279–83. Copyright ©1999 Massachusetts Medical Society. All rights reserved.

referral, they had the same aggregate odds—9.6 to 1. However, when black males (who had the same rate of referral as whites) were combined with black females (who had a lower rate of referral), the overall odds for all blacks were lower—5.5 to 1. Similarly, the aggregate odds for all males (black and white) were higher than the aggregate odds for all women.

So far, we have been talking about the *odds* of being referred for cardiac catheterization. But the researchers reported the *odds ratios*.[22] This slightly more complicated statistic involves a second stage of calculation (see the third column in Table 3). For example, the ratio of the odds of males being referred (9.6) to the odds of females being referred (5.5) is 1 to 0.6 (5.5/9.6 = 0.6). (Similarly, the ratio of the odds of whites being referred [9.6] to the odds of blacks being referred [5.5] is 1 to 0.6 [Table 3 shows this ratio as simply 0.6].) Odds ratios, like net additions to the workforce, are statistics which lack intuitively obvious meaning. Most people don't think in terms of odds ratios, nor do they understand what the term means.

Certainly this was true for the reporters who announced that blacks and women were only "60 percent as likely" to receive heart testing as whites and men. They misunderstood the odds ratio (0.6) to mean the relative likelihood of receiving the procedure. This was wrong. The correct comparison would have involved calculating the *risk ratios*, that is, figuring the relative chance, or risk, of being referred for testing. If 90.6 percent of whites and 84.7 percent of blacks are referred, then blacks are 93 percent as likely (84.7/90.6 = .93) to get referrals (see the fourth column in Table 3). That is, blacks were 93 percent as likely to be referred as whites, and women 93 percent as likely as men. Blacks and women, then, were not 40 percent less likely to receive referrals; they were 7 percent less likely to be referred.

As in the case of *Workforce 2000*, the misinterpretation of the results of this study began by mangling a poorly understood statistic. Reporters tried to translate the unfamiliar notion of odds ratios into more familiar statements of probability, and their resulting claims (blacks and women were 40 percent less likely to receive referrals) were simply wrong. Two other aspects of this case deserve mention. First, the researchers' decision to compare grouped data for males and females (and blacks with whites) distorted the nature of their findings. Remember that white males, black males, and white females had exactly the same rates of referrals. The use of aggregate comparisons obscured the real pattern (that only black females were referred at lower rates). Rather than suggesting that all women or all blacks were less likely to receive referrals, the researchers should have emphasized that black women received different recommendations from all other patients.

Second, we might wonder about the significance of receiving those referrals. The press reports simply assumed that referrals for cardiac catheterization (an invasive medical procedure that carries its own risks) were always appropriate, in effect implying that every patient should have received a referral. But perhaps this is wrong. Perhaps the study showed that physicians were too quick to refer males and white women for a risky procedure—but the press reports never considered this possibility. (The press also tended to forget that the doctors in this study were examining fictitious files, not treating real patients.)

The ease with which somewhat complex statistics can produce confusion is important, because we live in a world in which complex numbers are becoming more common. Simple statistical ideas—fractions, percentages, rates—are reasonably well understood by many people. But many social problems involve complex chains of cause and effect that can be understood only through complicated models developed by experts. Thus, current understandings for why some people develop heart disease or cancer assume that heredity plays a part, that various behaviors (diet, exercise, smoking, and so on) play roles, and that the environment has an influence. Sorting out the interconnected causes of these problems requires relatively complicated statistical ideas—net additions, odds ratios, and the like. If we have an imperfect understanding of these ideas, and if the reporters and other people who relay the statistics to us share our confusion—and they probably do—the chances are good that we'll soon be hearing—and repeating, and perhaps making decisions on the basis of—mutated statistics.

COMPOUND ERRORS:
CREATING CHAINS OF BAD STATISTICS

I have suggested that bad statistics often take on a life of their own. Rarely criticized, they gain widespread acceptance, and they are repeated over and over. Each repetition makes the number seem more credible—after all, everyone agrees that that's the correct figure. And, of course, bad statistics can become worse through mutation: through misuse or misunderstanding, the number becomes further distorted. But that's not the end of the process. Bad statistics can have additional ramifications when they become the basis for calculating still more statistics.

We can think about this process as compounding errors into a chain of bad statistics: one questionable number becomes the basis for a second statistic that is, in turn, flawed; and the process can continue as the second bad number leads to a third, and so on—each number a link in a chain of errors.

Consider, for example, some of the uses to which the Kinsey Reports have been put. During the 1930s and 1940s, the biologist Alfred Kinsey and his colleagues conducted lengthy interviews with several thousand people about their sexual experiences. These interviews became the basis for two books: *Sexual Behavior in the Human Male* (1948) and *Sexual Behavior in the Human Female* (1953), popularly known as the "Kinsey Reports."[23] The books challenged the polite fiction that most sex was confined to marriage; they revealed that many people had experience with a wide range of sexual behaviors, such as masturbation and premarital sex. However, the Kinsey data could not provide accurate estimates for the incidence of different sexual behaviors. While the thousands of interviews constituted a large sample, that sample was not representative, let alone random. The sample contained a much higher proportion of college-educated people than the general population and, in an effort to

MUTANT STATISTICS

explore a broad range of sexual experiences, Kinsey deliberately arranged interviews with a substantial number of active homosexuals, as well as with many individuals who had been imprisoned. Nonetheless, commentators sometimes treat the Kinsey findings as though they offer an authoritative, representative portrait of the American population. For example, gay and lesbian activists sometimes argue that one-tenth of the population is homosexual, and they refer to the Kinsey Reports to support this claim.

Rather than define heterosexual and homosexual as a simple dichotomy, the Kinsey Reports described a continuum that ranged from individuals who had never had a homosexual experience, to those who had some incidental homosexual experiences, and so on through those whose sexual experiences had been exclusively homosexual. Still, the male report estimated that "10 per cent of the males are more or less exclusively homosexual . . . for at least three years between the ages of 16 and 55."[24] (Later surveys, based on more representative samples, have concluded that the one-in-ten estimate exaggerated the amount of homosexuality; typically, they find that 3–6 percent of males [and a lower percentage of females] have had significant homosexual experience at some point in their lives [usually in adolescence or early adulthood], and that the incidence of homosexuality among adults is lower—between 1 and 3 percent.)[25] However, gay and lesbian activists often dispute these lower estimates; they prefer the one-in-ten figure because it suggests that homosexuals are a substantial minority group, roughly equal in number to African Americans—too large to be ignored. Thus, the 10 percent figure lives on, and it is often used in calculating other, new statistics about gays and lesbians.

Consider, for example, claims that one-third of teen suicides—or roughly 1,500 deaths per year—involve gay or lesbian adolescents. Gay activists invoked this statistic to portray the hardships gay and lesbian youth confront; it suggests that stigma and social isolation are severe enough to drive many adolescents to kill themselves.[26]

But how could anyone hope to measure gay teen suicides accurately? Many gays and lesbians try to conceal their sexual orientation, and certainly some teenagers might feel driven to suicide because keeping that secret was becoming a burden. But, given this secrecy, how could anyone know just which teenagers who commit suicide are gay or lesbian? Coroners, after all, do not record sexual orientation on death certificates.

So how did advocates arrive at the statistic that one-third of teenagers who kill themselves are homosexual? The answer is that they constructed a chain of bad statistics. They began with the familiar, Kinsey-based claim that one-tenth of the population—including, presumably, one-tenth of teenagers—is homosexual. Roughly 4,500 teenage deaths are attributed to suicide each year; on average, then, 10 percent of those—450 suicides—should involve gay or lesbian teens. (Note that we have already incorporated our first dubious statistic—derived from Kinsey's questionable sample—that 10 percent of the population is gay or lesbian.)

Next, advocates drew upon various studies that suggested that homosexuals attempted suicide at a rate two to three times

higher than heterosexuals. Note that this figure presumes knowledge about the rates of an often secretive behavior in two populations—one itself often hidden. Multiplying 10 percent (the estimated proportion of homosexuals in the population) by 3 (a
suicide rate estimated to be three times higher than that of heterosexuals) led to an estimate that gays and lesbians accounted
for 30 percent of suicides—and this figure was in turn rounded
up to one-third.* Thus, one-third of 4,500 teen suicides—1,500
deaths—involve gay or lesbian youths.

Notice how the final figure depends on the advocates'
assumptions. If the proportion of homosexuals among all teenagers is estimated at 3 percent, or 6 percent, the number of gay
teen suicides falls. If the rate at which homosexual teens commit
suicide is only twice that of heterosexuals, the number falls. (For
example, if we instead assume that 3 percent of the adolescent
population is gay or lesbian, and that their suicide rate is twice
that of heterosexuals, homosexuals would account for less than
6 percent of all teen suicides.) The final figure depends completely on the assumptions used to make the calculations.

This example offers two important lessons. The first is a

* There is another innumerate error hidden here. *Even if* 10 percent of the population is homosexual, and their suicide rate is three
times that of heterosexuals, homosexuals should account for only
one-quarter—not one-third—of suicides. Let Z be the suicide rate
for heterosexuals; if: (.1 [the proportion of the population that is
homosexual] $\times 3Z$) + (.9 [the proportion of the population that is het-
erosexual] $\times Z$) = 4,500 (the total number of teen suicides), then: (.1 $\times$
$3Z$) = 1,125 = one-quarter of 4,500.

reminder that bad statistics can live on. Most social scientists consider Kinsey's 10 percent estimate for homosexuality too high; more recent, more reliable studies have consistently produced lower estimates. Yet some gay and lesbian activists continue to cite the higher figure—precisely because it is the largest available number. In turn, 10 percent often figures into other calculations—not just about gay teen suicides, but also regarding the number of gay voters, the size of the gay population at risk of AIDS, and so on.

The second lesson is perhaps harder to learn. Any claim about the number of gay teen suicides should set off alarm bells. Given the difficulties in learning which deaths are suicides and which teenagers are gay, it obviously would be hard to learn the number of gay teen suicides. It is not unreasonable to ask how the advocates arrived at that number, and which assumptions lay behind their calculations. Those assumptions may be perfectly defensible, but they deserve to be examined. But, of course, such examinations are the exception, not the rule. Once offered, a statistic—such as the claim that gays and lesbians account for one-third of all teen suicides—tends to be repeated, to circulate widely, without confronting questions about its validity.

Compound errors can begin with any of the standard sorts of bad statistics—a guess, a poor sample, an inadvertent transformation, perhaps confusion over the meaning of a complex statistic. People inevitably want to put statistics to use, to explore a number's implications. An estimate for the number of homeless persons can help us predict the costs of social services for the homeless, just as an estimate of the proportion of the population that is homosexual lets us predict the number of gay and lesbian teenagers who may attempt suicide. But, when the original numbers are bad—and we have already explored some of the many ways bad numbers can come into circulation—compound errors can result. Assessing such statistics requires another level of critical thinking: one must ask both how advocates produced the statistic at hand (1,500 gay teen suicides), and whether they based their calculations on earlier numbers that are themselves questionable (e.g., 10 percent of the population is homosexual). The strengths and weaknesses of those original numbers should affect our confidence in the second-generation statistics.

THE ROOTS OF MUTANT STATISTICS

The problems addressed in chapter 2—guessing and troubles with definitions, measurement, and sampling—are relatively straightforward and easy to spot. However, detecting mutant statistics often requires tracing the history of a number, learning how its meaning or use changes over time. Mutant statistics don't always start out bad. Although a bad statistic often provides an excellent basis for mutation, even good statistics can be mangled into bad mutations.

There are several sources for mutation. *Innumeracy* is fundamental to the process. When people do not understand a statistic—how it came into being or what it means—they can make honest errors. They may try simply to repeat a number, but fail, inadvertently transforming the figure's meaning. More complicated statistics invite what we've called confusion or compound errors; the less obvious a number's meaning, the easier it is to mangle that meaning.

Mutant statistics are not necessarily evidence of dishonesty. Many advocates are perfectly sincere, yet innumerate. Their conviction that the problem is serious, that they need to make that seriousness clear to others, and that some statistic offers a means to do just that, coupled with their misunderstanding of how the numbers were arrived at or what they actually mean, provides the foundation for many of the sorts of errors detailed in this chapter.

However, there is also deliberate *manipulation*, conscious attempts to turn statistical information to particular uses. Data can be presented in ways that convey different impressions, and it is not uncommon for advocates to choose selectively which numbers they report, and to pick the words they use to describe the figures with care. That is, some numbers are selected because they promise to persuade, to support the advocates' positions. This need not be dishonest; advocates making a case can make it clear that they've chosen to interpret statistics in particular ways. But very often the questionable interpretive work remains hidden, and we have every reason to be suspicious of both the numbers and the advocates' honesty when mutations are concealed from the audience.

Whether they are sincere or cynical, advocates prefer dramatic statistics, numbers that make the problem seem as serious—and the need as urgent—as possible. The more dramatic a number's implications, the more likely it will be repeated. If transformation or confusion or compound error produces a mutant statistic that is more dramatic than the original figure, there is a good chance that the mutation will spread. Once in circulation, a mutant statistic is difficult to retract. People are much more likely to repeat a number (perhaps accidently transforming it yet again) than they are to stop and critically examine it. This is particularly true when the statistic seems dramatic; the drama ensures repetition, while innumeracy discourages critical thinking.

4

APPLES AND ORANGES

Inappropriate Comparisons

The newspaper story reported that, during the first six months of 2000, 56 people had died in traffic accidents in Delaware (the state where I live). Obviously, these deaths were tragedies for the families and friends of the people who died. But is 56 a lot of traffic deaths, a number that should be a focus of public concern? The story featured a chart contrasting the 56 deaths during the first half of 2000 with 1999's total of 104 traffic deaths. This implied that, if traffic deaths continued at the same pace during the second half of 2000, then the total—112 deaths—would represent an increase over the previous year. This might suggest that 56 was a lot of deaths—evidence of a growing problem. But the chart also showed that there had been 148 deaths in 1997 and 116 in 1998, suggesting that even 112 deaths might not be all that high a total.[1]

This example reveals that it is often hard to know how to interpret lone statistics, single numbers presented in isolation. Are 56 traffic deaths a cause for concern because they reveal a growing problem, or should the number be celebrated as evidence of improving traffic safety? By itself, the total of 56 deaths is hard to interpret. To make sense of this number, we must compare it to other figures—to the death totals in Delaware in other years or perhaps to traffic fatalities in other states (although we'd need to find some way of taking Delaware's small size into account—with fewer drivers and fewer miles of road, we would expect it to have many fewer deaths than, say, California or New York).

Such comparisons among numbers are essential to understanding most statistics. Comparison lets us put figures in some sort of context. The most obvious comparisons involve statistics from two different times (such as traffic deaths in two years) to measure whether things have somehow changed. (Of course, claims about social problems usually suggest that things have gotten worse, not better.) Other comparisons involve different places (comparing traffic death rates in different states or different countries), different groups (comparing traffic death rates among different age or ethnic groups), or even different social problems (how does the number of traffic fatalities compare to the numbers of deaths from other causes?). Such comparisons are necessary, but they also offer special opportunities for creating bad statistics. Some comparisons are better than others. The familiar warning against "comparing apples and oranges" reminds us of the dangers of inappropriate comparisons.

Good comparisons involve comparable items; they pair apples with apples, and oranges with oranges. Comparable statistics count the same things in the same ways. Comparisons among statistics that are not comparable confuse and distort. Before accepting any statistical comparison, it is important to ask whether the numbers are comparable. Unfortunately, finding comparable numbers can be tricky. Many comparisons that seem appropriate at first glance turn out to have serious flaws: numbers that might seem comparable in fact should not be compared. What at first glance seems to be all apples turns out to be mixed fruit.

COMPARISONS OVER TIME

We often hear warnings that some social problem is "epidemic." This expression suggests that the problem's growth is rapid, widespread, and out of control. If things are getting worse, and particularly if they're getting worse fast, we need to act.

Evidence that a social problem is getting worse depends on measuring the change in some social condition over at least two points in time: at Time A, the problem was this bad; at (later) Time B, it was that much worse.* Usually, there is an implication

*Note that we begin by assuming that someone has actually measured the social condition at two points in time. This need not be true. Since the early 1980s, a wide range of politicians and commentators have contrasted lists of the public schools' top problems in the 1940s (1. talking; 2. chewing gum; 3. making noise; etc.) with the top contemporary problems (1. drug abuse; 2. alcohol abuse; 3. pregnancy; etc.). While the format—two contrasting ranked lists—implies that someone conducted research (perhaps surveys of teachers?) in different

APPLES AND ORANGES

that things will continue to deteriorate, that the change for the worse is a trend.

If we want to measure change, we have to make comparisons over time, and statistics can help us make these comparisons. However, when we compare measures of some social problem at two different times, we need to remember that differences between two measurements need not reflect actual changes in the social problem; the way we measure the social problem may also change, and changes in measurement can drastically affect the resulting statistical comparison.

Changing Measures

Consider child abuse. Child advocates sometimes cite statistics showing that child abuse cases soared in the decades following the 1960s. For example, there were about 150,000 abused children reported in 1963, but nearly three million in 1995.[2] Such statistics seem to prove that child abuse became much more common during those years, but this simple interpretation ignores important changes in the way Americans defined and dealt with child abuse. In the early 1960s, experts, officials, and the mass

_____

years, this was not the case. As T. Cullen Davis, the Christian fundamentalist who originated the lists, explained: "They weren't done from a scientific survey. How did I know what the offenses in the schools were in 1940? I was there. How do I know what they are now? I read the newspapers" (Barry O'Neill, "The History of a Hoax," _New York Times Magazine,_ March 6, 1994, p.48). Guessing, then, can be the basis for comparisons, just as for other statistics.

media began drawing attention to the "battered child syndrome," and the term "child abuse" came into widespread use. Advocates initially focused on physicians' failures to report suspicious injuries to the authorities; legislators held hearings on the problem and passed a series of increasingly tough laws requiring that doctors—and later nurses, teachers, day-care workers, and other people who dealt with children—report all cases of suspected abuse. Training programs spread information about potential signs of abuse, so that these people would recognize cases that ought to be reported. In addition, the definition of abuse grew broader. Experts warned that abuse involved much more than beatings; it also included neglect, sexual abuse, emotional abuse, and so on. In other words, more people were required to report more kinds of abuse. Predictably, reported abuse rose dramatically.

Before 1960, then, the vast majority of what we now consider child abuse went unreported. But two changes reduced that very large dark figure: the definition of child abuse expanded to include a broader range of harms suffered by children; and the organizational practices that produced child-abuse reports changed once laws required professionals to report cases. Both changes should have increased the proportion of cases reported and reduced the dark figure.* Previously, for example, children

*Remember that, even as the dark figure grows smaller, reporting will never be perfect, and some cases of abuse will continue to go unreported. These false negatives (children whose suffering goes unrecognized) can justify advocates' calls for still broader definitions

brought to a hospital emergency room with suspicious injuries might have been treated and sent home; however, the new laws required reporting suspicious cases—and with broader definitions of abuse, more and more cases qualified as suspicious. So how should we interpret statistics showing a dramatic increase in child-abuse cases? Do they reveal a real increase in abuse? Or do they simply reflect new social arrangements that generate more reports of abuse? When there are significantly different methods for counting cases at two different times, comparisons become difficult to interpret.

The same pattern occurs after nearly every successful campaign to draw attention to a new social problem. Whenever a previously ignored social condition becomes defined as a serious social problem, and people begin to worry about it and try to solve the problem, they also begin keeping better records and, as a result, statistics for that problem show a sharp rise. In most cases, this need not mean that the problem is getting worse; rather, the statistical change reflects the fact that people now consider the problem worth reporting and important enough to deserve more accurate records. The statistics do not measure changes in the incidence of the problem so much as changes in social attitudes toward that problem and the organizational

---

of abuse and even tougher requirements for reporting cases. If those claims lead to new policies, the number of reported cases will of course rise further, and this evidence of increasing, epidemic child abuse can inspire additional calls for action. In theory, this cycle can continue indefinitely.

practices of the agencies that keep track of it. (However, activists often point to such statistics as evidence that the problem is getting worse, and argue that even more needs to be done to address the problem.)

In some cases, changes in measurements are deliberate. Since 1972, the Department of Justice has conducted National Crime Victimization Surveys (NCVS) to learn what proportion of the population has been victimized by crime. After critics argued that the NCVS's questions did not do enough to encourage respondents to report victimization, the survey was redesigned to reduce false negatives. New questions encouraged people to recall more victimization episodes and to understand the full range of incidents that ought to be reported (in particular, the redesigned survey was intended to elicit more complete reporting of sexual assaults and other crimes committed by intimates and family members).[3] Officials anticipated that the redesigned survey would lead to increased reports of victimization, and they were correct. (In particular, the new survey elicited far more reports of rape and sexual assaults.) The redesigned NCVS reduced crime's dark figure by eliciting more complete reporting by victims. However, the levels of victimization reported in the old and new surveys were not comparable, because the way victimization was measured had changed. Researchers at the Department of Justice understood this, and their reports were careful to recalculate the responses to the earlier surveys in an effort to make the data comparable. However, someone who did not understand how the NCVS had changed and who simply compared victimization rates from the old and new surveys could easily misinterpret the results and conclude that the sudden increase in reported victimization reflected an increase in the level of crime, rather than merely a change in how victimization was measured.

Unchanging Measures

Changing measures are a particularly common problem with comparisons over time, but unchanging measures also can cause problems of their own. This occurs when changes in the larger society make an established measure less accurate or less meaningful.* For example, in the late 1940s, the federal Bureau of Labor Statistics (BLS) began publishing quarterly reports measuring economic productivity (basically this statistic involved dividing the value of the goods produced in the economy by the total hours people worked—when the value of goods produced per hour of work rises, productivity increases).[4] These figures quickly became of more than academic interest; management and labor unions in major industries agreed to labor contracts that tied rising wages to increased productivity as measured by the BLS. Powerful interests now had a stake in how productivity was measured, and the BLS formula became institutionalized. That is, management would resist any change in the formula that would show increased productivity (and therefore justify higher wages for workers), while unions would resist any change that would

---

*The most familiar example is the way inflation alters the value of money over time. Thus, economists are careful to take this into account by calculating sums for different years in "constant dollars."

reveal lower productivity (and suppress wage increases). However, as the economy evolved, critics argued that the formula was becoming outdated. For example, the formula had particular difficulty measuring productivity in service industries, yet services were a growing proportion of the economy. In the 1970s, productivity fell markedly, but critics argued that much of that decline reflected the failure of the BLS formula to measure economic activity accurately in a transformed economy.

This example reminds us of a basic lesson from chapter 2: measurement involves making choices. All measures have limitations, and there may be good reasons to alter measures to make them more accurate. But improving measurement will probably affect the resulting statistics. We need to be especially careful when we try to compare statistics produced by old measures with those resulting from new, improved measures, because changing statistics then may reflect shifting measurement choices, rather than changes in the nature of the social problem. Yet we also need to be wary of unchanging measures that may become less accurate as the social conditions they are supposed to measure shift.

Projections

Another form of comparison across time contrasts the present with the future. Obviously, we cannot know precisely what the future holds, but we can make projections. In some cases, we can have great confidence in our projections. If all—or virtually all—births and deaths are recorded each year, the number of births in this year's cohort offers a good basis for projecting the number of five-year-olds who will start kindergarten five years from now. We will have to predict how many children in the cohort will die, and how many will be added through immigration and subtracted through emigration, and the accuracy of our prediction will depend on how well we can estimate those changes in the cohort's population. But a society that keeps good track of births probably also has good death records, and childhood death rates probably won't vary too much from year to year, so our prediction should be reasonably accurate.

The value of predictive social statistics, then, depends on how they are calculated. There are two reasons it is relatively easy to predict the number of kindergarten students in five years. First, the prediction is based on an initial estimate (birth records) that we consider relatively complete and accurate because physicians, midwives, and hospitals are required to file birth certificates. Second, because we have been keeping population records for a long time, and because these records rarely show abrupt year-to-year fluctuations, we can assume that we have a pretty good understanding of the factors that might affect our cohort's size over the next few years. (We can make analogous predictions for the number of 20-year-olds in twenty years, the number of 70-year-olds in seventy years, and so on, although we inevitably have less confidence in the accuracy of these predictions the further they forecast into the future.)

However, not all projections are grounded in solid data and informed by a good understanding of the factors likely to shape the future. Consider, for example, the early, alarmist predictions about the future of "crack babies." Crack came to widespread public attention suddenly, in 1986. Warnings that this was an especially dangerous drug spread from a broad array of officials, experts, activists, and media sources; many of these warnings focused on the plight of babies born to mothers who used crack.[5] Supposedly addicted at birth, these infants were reported to display various medical and behavioral problems; for example, they tended to be underweight and irritable. Some physicians warned that crack babies had suffered irreparable biological harm, that they would continue to suffer a variety of medical, psychological, and behavioral problems, that many would be permanently retarded, that they would require special education services when they reached school age, and that they would be a perpetual drain on society's social services. Advocates warned that there might be 375,000 crack babies born each year, and that they might cost society—here estimates varied a good deal—$500 million or $3 billion or $20 billion annually. Crack, then, was denounced not only for the usual reasons illegal drugs come under attack, but also because crack babies promised to become an enduring legacy of social harm.

However, as time passed and the crack babies grew older, it became obvious that this costly legacy had been exaggerated. The advocates' claims involved two errors. First, they badly overestimated the number of crack babies; later studies placed the annual number of births at 30,000 to 50,000—roughly one-tenth the earlier estimate. Second, crack babies did not exhibit the kinds of unique, permanent damage that had been predicted. This is not to say that they did not have problems. Because mothers addicted to crack tended to be impoverished, they often had poor nutrition and inadequate medical care during their pregnancies, and their babies faced considerable disadvantages. But children born addicted to crack did not have more severe problems than other, nonaddicted children born in similar circumstances. Of course, poverty has serious effects on children's lives and prospects, but crack did not add huge special burdens. The early projections had been based on inaccurate assumptions, and they proved to be poor predictions.

Early predictions about the spread of AIDS had similar flaws. First identified in the early 1980s, AIDS posed a frightening, uncertain threat. Statistics on infections showed rapidly increasing numbers of cases—increases that reflected not only the disease's spread, but growing awareness of the disease, so that medical professionals were more likely to suspect and diagnose AIDS (and the definition for classifying cases also became broader). There was great concern about the future spread of the disease, particularly once the media publicized claims that AIDS might spread throughout the general population.[6] So long as transmission seemed confined to gay males, intravenous drug users, and hemophiliacs, the great majority of the population might consider themselves effectively immune from infection. However, by the mid-1980s, warnings that AIDS might be spread through heterosexual intercourse—or even insect bites—encouraged all people to consider themselves at risk. The news media found that the threat of heterosexually transmitted AIDS made a more compelling news story, and AIDS activists recognized that broad public concern could help them garner more support for research and treatment aimed at eliminating the threat of AIDS.

These concerns set the stage for predictions that emphasized the prospective spread of AIDS. For example, a 1987 article in a major newsmagazine predicted there might be ten million Americans infected with HIV by 1991 (the actual number of infections reported by 1991, according to the Centers for Disease Control, proved to be about 200,000). Such predictions were based on several erroneous assumptions, especially exaggerated estimates for the proportion of homosexuals in the population (another misuse of the Kinsey Report's 10 percent figure—see chapter 3) and for the ease with which AIDS could be transmitted through heterosexual intercourse. Coupling big numbers with claims that no sexually active person could be immune, advocates may have maximized public concern, but their predictions bore no resemblance to what would occur.

The examples of crack babies and AIDS illustrate a tendency to make exaggerated, worst-case projections regarding the spread of new social problems. This is, of course, another example of the power of big numbers. Frightening predictions make powerful media stories, and a lack of solid information about the spread of a new social problem, fear that the dark figure may be large, and advocates' sense of urgency make it especially easy to promote disturbing predictions.

We cannot talk about change without making comparisons over time. We cannot avoid such comparisons, nor should we want to. However, there are several basic problems that can affect statistics about change. It is important to consider the problems posed by changing—and sometimes unchanging—measures, and it is also important to recognize the limits of predictions. Claims about change deserve critical inspection; we need to ask ourselves whether apples are being compared to apples—or to very different objects.

COMPARISONS AMONG PLACES

Another standard sort of comparison is geographic; it compares statistics from different places. These might be numbers from places of the same sort—two or more cities, or states, regions, or countries—or they might involve comparisons of different kinds of places, such as rural and urban areas.

Geographic comparison is basic to much social science. Often it is made easy because bureaucracies have responsibility for keeping records within particular geographic jurisdictions, and it is relatively simple to compare those records. Thus, the FBI invites all law enforcement agencies to submit reports on crimes that have come to their attention; most agencies cooperate, and the FBI compiles its reports into its Uniform Crime Reports, calculating crime rates for the various states, counties, and cities.

Such comparisons depend on the different agencies producing comparable statistics. The FBI tries to guarantee this by providing detailed rules for reporting agencies; these rules seek to ensure that all agencies use the same definitions of crimes, as well as similar methods of measurement. Similar definitions and methods should produce numbers that are reasonably comparable—apples and apples.

But when agencies define phenomena in very different ways,

or use different methods of collecting statistical information, the resulting numbers cannot be meaningfully compared (recall chapter 3's discussion of the unreliability of early hate-crime statistics). Another example involves the records some urban police forces keep of "gang-related" homicides. But what makes a homicide gang-related? Police departments have devised very different answers to that question.[7] A department may choose to adopt a narrow definition; for example, labeling a homicide as gang-related only if the killer and the victim were known members of rival gangs *and* if gang rivalry is known to have been the motivation for the killing. In contrast, another police department may favor a broad definition, counting a homicide as "gang-related" if *either* the killer *or* the victim was *either* a gang member *or* associated with gang members, *regardless* of the motivation for the crime. The choice of definition makes a big difference. One study found that applying a broad definition identified twice as many gang-related homicides as a narrower definition. Depending upon circumstances, police departments might prefer to adopt either a broad definition (perhaps using the higher number of gang-related homicides to justify budget increases for an expanded antigang unit), or a narrow definition (presenting a lower number of gang-related homicides as evidence that the department is doing an effective job keeping gangs under control). The point is not that one definition is correct and the other is wrong, but rather that it is pointless to compare statistics collected using different definitions—the two definitions count different things, regardless of whether they both claim to be counting "gang-related" homicides.

Geographic comparisons become particularly troublesome when they involve different countries. Differences in language, culture, and social structure make international comparisons tricky, even when they seem straightforward. For example, critics sometimes argue that the United States has far more lawyers than other countries (usually implying that our oversupply of lawyers fosters excessive, senseless litigation).[8] This might seem like a straightforward comparison—surely everyone knows what a lawyer is, and it ought to be reasonably easy to count them. But those assumptions ignore international differences in the way the law is organized and administered. For example, Japan supposedly has far fewer lawyers (just over one per 10,000 population), while the United States has more than 28 lawyers for every 10,000 people. But what is meant by a lawyer? In the United States, lawyers are people who complete a law degree and pass the bar exam (and most people who take the exam pass it). In contrast, many Japanese receive law degrees, but less than 2 percent of them pass the exam that licenses them as *bengoshi* (individuals who can sell legal services). The vast majority of Japanese who receive law degrees provide in-house legal advice for government agencies and corporations, but they are not counted as lawyers, whereas attorneys in the United States who provide similar services are. The claim that the United States has far more lawyers than Japan depends on comparing the total of all U.S. lawyers with the number of Japanese bengoshi. A different definition—one that counts all non-bengoshi law graduates as Japanese lawyers—reveals that the United States and Japan have roughly similar proportions of lawyers (in 1987, these numbers were 28 and 32 per 10,000 people in the population, respectively). The question, then, becomes what is the most appropriate definition of a lawyer?

Similar problems bedevil international comparisons of educational achievement.[9] The media regularly report that U.S. students score less well on academic tests than their counterparts in other countries; in some cases, Americans are near—or even at—the bottom of the rankings. Such comparisons need to be interpreted with care, because the differences in scores may say more about differences in countries' educational systems than they do about students' abilities. For example, in the United States, virtually all young people attend high school (and around seven out of eight graduate). In contrast, in most other countries only the better students attend institutions equivalent to U.S. high schools (that is, schools that prepare students for admission to institutions of higher education); other students take different educational paths, such as into vocational education. International comparisons of high school students, then, sometimes contrast virtually all Americans (both the high-scoring better students and the low-scoring poorer students, producing an average score somewhere in the middle) with only the better students in other countries (who have relatively high average scores). The students in the different countries may take the same test, but if the samples of students being tested are very different, apples will again be compared to oranges.* Obviously,

---

*There are other problems with international comparisons of test scores. For example, American mathematics instruction tends to

APPLES AND ORANGES

the point is not that U.S. students are more or less able than students elsewhere—there is considerable debate over this issue—but that making such claims requires thinking carefully about the nature of the comparisons being made.

The basic problem with geographic comparisons, then, is that there is a good chance that statistics gathered from different places are based on different definitions and different measurements, so that they are not really comparable. Again, it is often desirable to make geographic comparisons, but we need to be cautious when interpreting those statistics.

COMPARISONS AMONG GROUPS

We can also compare different groups of people, such as people of different social classes, ethnic backgrounds, or religious affiliations. Arguing that groups somehow differ is another basic form of statistical analysis in the social sciences but, like comparisons across time and space, such arguments have common pitfalls.

Perhaps the most obvious problem involves comparing

---

place relatively more emphasis on problem-solving and less on computation, compared to mathematics instruction in some other countries. In tests that emphasize problem-solving, American students tend to do comparatively well; in tests that emphasize computation, they do relatively poorly. This is yet another case where the choice of measurement makes a difference.

groups of different sizes. Suppose, for example, that we hear that some new cult is the fastest growing religion in the country. Upon examining the numbers, we might find that last year the cult had 20 members, and this year it added 200 more—a 1,000 percent increase. Certainly this represents dramatic growth, and it is a rate of growth that larger, more established religious denominations certainly cannot match. There are, for example, roughly 60 million Roman Catholics in the United States. To grow 1,000 percent in one year, they would have to add 600 million members. (This new total—660 million Catholics—would outnumber the population of the entire country [some 270 million in 1998], an obvious impossibility.) On the other hand, it would not be a tremendous feat for Catholics to add another 200 members, even though the same increase in the number of members represents astonishing growth for our 20-person cult. As this example suggests, statistical comparisons of groups of very different sizes can be quite misleading.

Some statistical claims take advantage of differences in group size to emphasize particular aspects of social problems. Take, for example, discussions of race in the United States. The U.S. Bureau of the Census estimated that the U.S. population in 1996 was 82.9 percent white, 12.6 percent black, and 4.5 percent other (including Asians and Native Americans). This apparently simple classification is itself controversial for several reasons: it obviously oversimplifies by classifying each individual into a single racial category, even though a substantial proportion of the population has a mixed heritage; it ignores Hispanics or Latinos (the census bureau treats Hispanic as an ethnic, rather than a racial category, and classifies some Hispanics as white, some as black, and some as Native American); labels for racial categories shift over time (e.g., from Negro to black to African American); and so on.[10] The discussion that follows will ignore all these debates and simply focus on one point: whites outnumber blacks by more than six to one.

The fact that there are many more whites than blacks does not pose a problem for many statistical comparisons. We can, for example, compare averages in the two groups to show that, on average, whites have higher incomes, longer life expectancies, and so on. Comparing group averages, percentages within groups, or rates are simple ways of taking the groups' different sizes into account.

But we invite confusion when we compare *numbers of cases* from groups of very different sizes. Suppose someone makes the point: "Most poor people are white." Advocates sometimes use such statements to challenge stereotypes that portray the poor as black. But this claim is hardly surprising. If whites outnumber blacks by six to one, and poverty is distributed evenly across the population, then whites should outnumber blacks among the poor by six to one. Imagine 700 families—600 whites and 100 blacks. If 60 white families and 20 black families are poor, then poor white families obviously outnumber poor black families. But this comparison ignores the differences in the groups' sizes. If we compare the proportion of poor families in each group, we find that 10 percent (60 divided by 600) of white families are poor, compared to 20 percent of black families (20 divided by 100). While it is true that most poor families in this hypothetical example are white, this is not especially meaningful, because the difference in the size of the two groups makes it likely that whites will outnumber blacks in most categories. In such cases, it usually makes sense to compare percentages or rates within each group (so that, in our example, we see that the poverty rate among black families is twice as high as the rate among white families).

By choosing whether to report numbers or rates, advocates can convey very different impressions. Consider the data in Table 4 showing whites' and blacks' victimization and arrests for crimes of violence in 1997 (the victimization figures come from the National Crime Victimization Survey that asked people whether they'd been crime victims; the arrest figures come from law enforcement agencies' reports to the FBI). The table has three columns: the first gives the numbers of victimizations and arrests for each race (that is, an estimated 7,068,590 whites were victims of violent crimes, and so on); the second gives percentages (for instance, 82.1 percent of violent-crime victims were white, while blacks accounted for 15.2 percent of victims—the percentages in this column total less than 100 percent because some victimizations and arrests involve people of other races); and the third gives a rate (for example, for every 1,000 whites aged ten and above, there were 37.1 whites victimized by violent crimes). Now imagine two advocates: the first says, "Whites account for more than 80 percent of the victims of violent crime, yet blacks are arrested at a rate roughly five times greater than whites"; while the second advocate says, "Blacks are victimized at a rate more than 25 percent higher than whites, yet most people arrested for crimes of violence are white." Note that both

Table 4. *Comparing Whites' and Blacks' Victimizations and Arrests for Crimes of Violence, 1997*

	Number	Percent	Rate[a]
Victimization[b]			
Whites	7,068,590	82.1	37.1
Blacks	1,306,810	15.2	46.8
Arrests[c]			
Whites	284,523	56.8	1.5
Blacks	205,823	41.1	7.4

[a] Per 1,000 people aged 10 and above.

[b] Estimates for personal victimization (crimes of violence) derived from 1997 National Crime Victimization Survey.

[c] Arrests for violent crime reported in 1997 Uniform Crime Reports.

SOURCES: Kathleen Maguire and Ann L. Pastore, eds., *Sourcebook of Criminal Justice Statistics, 1998* (Washington, D.C.: Bureau of Justice Statistics, 1999), pp. 176, 342; U.S. Bureau of the Census, *Statistical Abstract of the United States: 1998*, 118th ed. (Washington, D.C., 1998), p. 14.

advocates are quite correct, yet they manage to convey very different (and distorted) impressions: the first implies that the crime problem is one of black criminals and white victims, the second that the crime problem involves white criminals and black victims. In each case, the advocate creates a distorted impression by contrasting an apple (a statistic that measures a group's percentage of the total—a number that is sensitive to the relative size of the groups) with an orange (a measure of a rate—one way of controlling for differences in group size). The lesson, then, is that we must keep differences in groups' sizes in mind when we make comparisons among groups. When groups are of significantly different size, we need to ask how statistics deal with that fact.

Comparing racial groups raises another issue. Most social scientists who compare whites and blacks do not assume that race in and of itself—that is, the biological differences among races—is especially important. Rather, they treat race as a crude measure of social class. Class itself is difficult to define and measure; most sociologists recognize that your class is related to how much money you have, how you came by that money, how much education you have, and so on. In general, whites and blacks differ on these measures: on average, whites have higher incomes, greater wealth, more education, and so on; and whites therefore have higher class standing, on average, than blacks. But bureaucracies routinely collect data on race, not class: schools classify students as white or black (but usually not as middle-class, working-class, or lower-class); police classify those they arrest by race but not class; and so on. As a practical matter, then, it is much simpler to contrast people of different races than people of different classes, but many differences among racial groups are really class differences, caused by differences in access to money, rather than differences in skin color.

Sorting out the effects of race and class requires statistics that measure both variables. For example, the data in Table 4 showed that blacks have higher arrest rates than whites. If only police col-

Table 5. *Hypothetical Data Showing How Apparent Racial*
Differences in Arrests Might Really Reflect Class Differences

100 white youths are arrested 10 times (arrest rate = 10 per 100 youths)	100 black youths are arrested 17 times (arrest rate = 17 per 100 youths)
80 middle-class white youths are arrested 4 times (arrest rate = 5 per 100 youths)	50 middle-class black youths are arrested 2 times (arrest rate = 4 per 100 youths)
20 lower-class white youths are arrested 6 times (arrest rate = 30 per 100 youths)	50 lower-class black youths are arrested 15 times (arrest rate = 30 per 100 youths)

lected information about the social class of those they arrest, we might reexamine these data while controlling for class. Table 5 offers hypothetical data for this sort of analysis. It presents an imaginary comparison between 100 white youths and 100 black youths; in the example, there are 10 arrests for delinquent acts committed by the white youths (for a rate of 10 per 100 youths), and 17 arrests of black youths (a rate of 17 per 100). But suppose we divide each race into middle- and lower-class subgroups and then calculate arrest rates for middle-class whites, middle-class blacks, etc. Table 5 imagines that the 100 white youths include 80 middle-class youths (arrested 4 times—a rate of 5 per 100 [4 arrests/80 middle-class white youths]) and 20 lower-class youths (arrested 6 times—a rate of 30 per 100), but that the 100 black youths are evenly split by class: 50 are middle-class (2 arrests—a rate of 4 per 100), and 50 are lower-class (15 arrests—a rate of 30 per 100). This example reveals that apparently dramatic racial differences in rates of arrests for delinquency might disappear once we control for class: if a much larger proportion of whites than blacks is middle-class, and if middle-class people are arrested at much lower rates than lower-class people, then we might find that middle-class people of both races have equally low arrest rates, while the arrest rates for lower-class people of both races are equally high. (Again—the numbers in Table 5 are imaginary; they simply illustrate the principle that controlling for a third variable—in this case, social class—can be important.)

Although it is easy to create hypothetical examples, it is difficult to perform such analyses in practice. The required information usually is not available (for instance, police do not routinely report the class of those they arrest). Moreover, such comparisons, particularly when they control for more than one variable (suppose we wanted to control for age, gender, and other variables in addition to class), require advanced statistical techniques. But the underlying point is important. When we discover a difference between two groups (e.g., that blacks and whites have different arrest rates), it is easy to assume that the obvious difference between the groups (race) *causes* other differences (e.g., in arrest rates). It is always possible that something else, some other variable (such as class) actually causes the difference. (This is an important issue in philosophy: apparent relationships between two variables that are actually caused by a third variable are called *spurious*.) When we are told that two groups are different, rather than simply accepting that finding we ought to at least ask ourselves whether something else, some other variable, might account for the supposed difference.

Comparisons among groups can be tricky precisely because they seem so straightforward. Such claims deserve critical examination. Are the groups really comparable? Are they different in some way (such as their relative size) that affects the statistics used to make the comparison? Is there some other, unmentioned variable (such as class) that may affect the differences among groups? These are basic questions that deserve consideration whenever we compare groups.

COMPARISONS AMONG SOCIAL PROBLEMS

A fourth kind of comparison contrasts different social problems. Campaigns to draw attention to new social problems routinely argue that we have been ignoring something we ought to consider important, that we have been paying too much attention to other problems. In this sense, social problems claims are competitive. Advocates suspect that, if we worry more about one issue, we probably will worry less about another, and they work hard to keep us focused on the problem that concerns them.

In some cases, advocates refuse to compare social problems. They try to raise our concern by setting an absolute standard for measuring social harm ("You can't place a value on a human life!" "Even one victim is too many!"). But few social arrangements are risk-free. Roughly 40,000 Americans die annually in automobile accidents—twice the number that die in homicides, or about 20 times as many as die in airline crashes. Yet we take the risk of traffic accidents for granted, and we accept this level of risk. (When the national speed limit was lowered to 55 miles per hour in the 1970s, traffic deaths fell. Presumably they would have fallen further had the limit been set at 45, or 35; however, no one advocated such lower limits. As a society, we were willing to trade a certain death toll for the convenience of reasonably speedy travel. And, in the 1990s, when Congress raised speed limits, it acknowledged that the higher limits would lead to more deaths.) Yet, while we accept the (relatively high) risk of traffic fatalities, we worry about new technology—power lines or computer terminals or food additives—even though those who warn about technological risks usually offer far lower estimates for the number of people harmed by the new threat.

A similar logic underpins some people's reluctance to wear seat belts: "You could get in a crash," they say, "and instead of being thrown free of the car and surviving, you could be pinned in the wreckage by your seat belt and killed." No doubt this happens on occasion: some people wearing seat belts die in circumstances where, without a seat belt, they might have lived. On the other hand, far more people die each year because they were not wearing seat belts in circumstances where the belt might have saved them. In short, arguing that something *might* happen, that there is some small risk, is not enough. Too often, advocates present their claims in isolation. That is, they say, "This is a big problem," not "This problem is bigger than other problems." Claims about some new social problem ought to discuss the relative risks, in comparison to other problems.

In general, we worry more about more serious threats. We worry more about murder than we do about automobile theft.

This is not because murder is more common. It definitely is not; for every criminal homicide, there are nearly 70 motor vehicles stolen (in 1995, the FBI reported 21,600 murders and 1,472,700 vehicle thefts).[11] But murder is a much more serious crime, and it becomes the focus for our fears and concerns.

This raises an issue: How can we know which problems pose the most serious—or at least relatively serious—threats? The competition among social problems claims means that anyone promoting a social problem finds it useful to portray that problem as particularly serious, as meriting special attention and concern. The media are more likely to publicize problems that seem serious, officials usually give serious threats higher priority, and so on.

Statistics often play a role in these efforts to define new social problems as major threats. Several devices—including some that we've already examined—serve this purpose, including: big numbers (estimates that many people are affected suggest that a problem is serious); rapid increases (comparisons across time showing a rapidly growing problem make the situation seem urgent); and geographic and group comparisons (evidence that a problem is worse here than elsewhere [or worse within this group than in others] suggest that the problem need not be this bad—that something could be done).

The problem with comparing social problems is our familiar apples-and-oranges dilemma. Should we focus on monetary costs? On lives lost? On the number of people affected? On the nature of the threat? How should we compare threats? Is a disease that threatens the lives of infants more serious than one that threatens old people? Is a problem that threatens lives always more important than one that isn't life-threatening but impairs the quality of life or costs lots of money? (What if just a few lives are threatened, but vast amounts of money are at stake?) Making comparisons among social problems can be complicated, and this complexity encourages bad statistics.

One temptation is to estimate the dollar costs of various social problems. Advocates sometimes claim that a given social problem costs so many millions (or billions) per year. Such figures might seem comparable—if all costs are in dollars, we ought to be able to see that Problem A costs this much more than Problem B, and so on. But how is it possible to calculate such costs? The National Institute of Alcohol Abuse and Alcoholism (NIAAA) places alcoholism's annual costs to society in the hundreds of billions of dollars. The NIAAA produces these figures through a complicated formula that adds such costs as: the total cost of alcohol treatment programs; a portion of the costs of treating various diseases that alcoholism causes; the value of lost earnings due to reduced productivity (this one item accounts for more than half of the total costs); the costs of crimes caused by alcoholism; and so on. Each of these costs must be estimated using a special formula, and each formula must make various assumptions and estimates (for example, what proportions of different diseases or crimes are caused by alcoholism, and what the costs are of treating those diseases or dealing with those crimes). Producing the NIAAA's final cost figure, then, requires making dozens of assumptions, each of which might be debated. One attempt to analyze the NIAAA's cost figures concluded that the agency's formula was "strongly biased in the direction of overstating the costs."[12] This is not surprising; after all, as a government agency dedicated to addressing alcohol problems, the NIAAA has an interest in convincing Congress, the media, and the public that alcohol problems are important problems, and that it, therefore, is an important agency. Claims about the costs of social problems, then, are difficult to evaluate (breaking down a formula and critically examining each of its elements is time-consuming and almost always requires specialized knowledge). However, we should at least recognize that such numbers are imprecise, and that they offer many opportunities for advocates' assumptions and biases to shape the results.

Another flawed method of emphasizing a problem's importance is to focus on some narrowly defined population where the problem is relatively concentrated. Consider this claim from a scholarly article on teen suicide: "Suicide is the second leading cause of death among adolescents. . . ."[13] It is difficult to know how to evaluate this claim, because it does not define its terms: What is an adolescent? What are the other categories for cause of death?* But a key feature of this statistic is that it concerns only

* This statistic depends heavily on the classification of causes. In 1991, there were 15,313 deaths of people aged 15–19. Of these, 6,935 (45 percent) died in accidents, 3,365 (22 percent) in homicides, 2,964 (19 percent) from various diseases, and only 1,899 (12 percent) in suicides (*Vital Statistics of the United States, 1991. Vol. II—Mortality, Part A* [Washington, D. C., 1996], Table 1-27, pp. 132–71). In order to argue that suicide is the second-leading cause of death, it is necessary to subdivide these other categories (so that, for example, rather

adolescents. Adolescents have a much lower death rate than adults, primarily because few adolescents die from heart disease, cancer, strokes, and the other diseases that account for most deaths. Infants and adults—especially older adults—are far more likely to suffer fatal diseases than adolescents, and this shapes overall death rates. In other words, because relatively few adolescents die each year, it doesn't take all that many deaths to account for a large share of adolescent deaths. (Similarly, in assessing warnings that AIDS accounts for a large share of deaths among males in their twenties, it is important to remember that relatively few males in that age group die from other causes.) Thus, an age group rarely beset by other causes of death is the perfect population for emphasizing the importance of some lethal threat.

The flaws that characterize attempts to rank social problems, or to calculate their costs, remind us of some basic lessons. Advocates for particular problems find themselves competing for society's attention and concern. Most advocates feel committed to their problem; they believe it is important, that solving it ought to be a priority. They look for statistics that support their position, evidence that can persuade others to do what they want. But campaigns to arouse concern about one issue threaten to make us lose sight of other issues—issues that are more familiar, but that also may pose bigger threats. Comparing social

---

than considering accidents or disease as general categories of death, different types of accidents and specific diseases are each classified as distinct causes of death)—or we might lump all other deaths into a single category.

problems to one another, then, is useful—so long as we remember to compare apples to apples.

THE LOGIC OF COMPARISON

For a variety of reasons, contemporary society tends to focus on social problems one at a time. Most activists campaign to draw attention to a particular issue. The media prefer to cover stories one by one. Researchers find it easier to study specific topics. As a result, we tend to think about individual social problems, instead of looking at their larger social context. The most common social problems statistics reflect this tendency. A lone figure ("It's a big number!") serves to demonstrate a problem's size. There is no overt comparison; it is all implicit, if there's a big number, there must be a big problem.

Statistical comparisons promise a bit more—at least two numbers that might reveal a pattern: things are getting worse; or things are worse in one place than another; or this group has it worse than that one; or even this problem is more important than some others. But comparison depends on comparability. Unless each number reflects the same definitions and the same methods of measurement—unless each number is an apple, and not something else—comparisons can be deceptive. Unless the numbers are comparable, the pattern apparently revealed through comparison may say more about the nature of the numbers than it does about the nature of the social problem.

5

STAT WARS

Conflicts over Social Statistics

In the early 1980s, missing children became a prominent social problem; their faces appeared on milk cartons, and their stories were featured on television specials. Advocates coupled frightening examples of murdered or vanished children with disturbing statistics: strangers, they claimed, kidnapped 50,000 children each year. In 1985, reporters at the *Denver Post* won a Pulitzer Prize for pointing out that the movement's statistics were exaggerated: they identified a "numbers gap" between the 50,000 estimate and the roughly 70 child kidnappings investigated annually by the FBI. In response, one activist testified before Congress: "I don't think anything has surprised me more than this preoccupation with numbers, and the . . . 'only 67 or 68 or only 69.' . . . What is it with the 'only,' sir?" A movement that had promoted big numbers now argued that smaller, more accurate numbers were irrelevant. [1]

All too often, bad statistics endure because no one questions them and points out their flaws. Any number—even the most implausible figure (for example, 50,000 stranger abductions)—can survive if it goes unchallenged. We have identified the key issues in evaluating statistics: How did they arrive at that number? Is the number being used properly? Are the appropriate comparisons being made? While these issues aren't all that difficult to understand, many of us seem intimidated when faced with almost any statistic. Rather than ask the obvious questions, we tend to remain silent. As a result, bad statistics can take on a life of their own; they survive and even thrive.

But not always. Some statistics—such as the number of children abducted by strangers—lead to public controversies, open debates over numbers and their interpretation. We are told that guns kept in the home are rarely—no, frequently—used in self-defense, that they often—no, only rarely—kill family members. Environmentalist scientists estimate that water contaminated by nuclear power plants will cause many cancer deaths; scientists employed by the power industry insist that such deaths will be very rare. Such *stat wars* also intimidate us. If it is hard to evaluate one number, how can we be expected to assess the relative merits of different, competing statistics?

Stat wars indicate that someone cares enough to dispute a statistic. Usually these debates reflect the opponents' competing interests. In chapter 1, we noted that statistics can become weapons in political and social debates. People who make claims about social problems have goals: they hope to convince others that they have identified a particular problem, that the problem is serious and deserves attention, that they understand the problem's causes, and that they know how to solve it. Those whose claims succeed in convincing others stand to benefit. These benefits may include influencing social policy—perhaps by getting a new law passed, or a new program funded—but they go beyond that. People who make successful claims are likely to gain influence, power, status, even money; they become more important. Therefore, advocates usually have a vested interest in the success of their claims—whatever sincere commitment they have to their cause, they also stand to gain personally if their claims convince others.

In addition to advancing their personal beliefs and interests, people present claims that promote the interests of their groups. For decades, the tobacco industry insisted that there was no convincing evidence that cigarette smoking caused disease. Obviously, those claims reflected the industry's bedrock economic interests: if tobacco were harmless, the tobacco industry should be able to continue selling it and profiting from its sale; if tobacco were harmless, the industry was justified in resisting every effort to restrict its business and therefore its profits; if tobacco were harmless, the industry should not be held liable for any harms suffered by smokers. While this example is particularly blatant, claims often reflect underlying interests of the individuals and groups who make them.

Often advocates find themselves struggling against others with competing interests: Republicans and Democrats oppose one another in political races; liberals and conservatives clash over the direction of public policy; corporations compete with one another to control markets; and on and on. Even activists debate the tactics and priorities of their social movements. Outsiders struggle to become insiders, while insiders try to keep them out; the have-nots want to get theirs, while the haves want more. These competing interests foster competing claims, and competing claims often lead to competing statistics.

We should expect people to promote statistics that support their interests. This need not be dishonest or cynical. Most people believe that their interests are legitimate, that their cause is just. They seize upon whatever evidence supports their position, and they point to it with pride and conviction. Often, this evidence is statistical. Remember that contemporary society tends to treat numbers with respect; statistics seem to offer hard, factual, indisputable evidence. When people find numbers that seem to support what they believe—and their interests—they tend to accept them. Recall chapter 2's discussion of the ease with which activists produce, believe in, and justify big estimates for the size of social problems. It is especially difficult for most of us to think critically about statistics that seem to confirm what we already believe to be true. We may question the definitions, the measurements, or the samples that lie behind statistics offered by our opponents, but we are less likely to ask the same sorts of questions about figures that seem to support our own positions. Our numbers are undoubtedly good numbers, while our opponents' figures are questionable at best.

Precisely because our society treats statistics as a powerful form of evidence, competing interests often lead to conflicts over statistics—to stat wars. If one group offers statistics ("These are facts!") to support its position, its competitors are likely to feel pressured to find other numbers that support their interests. At times, debates over whose numbers are more accurate attract media attention. This is risky. If the media treat one side's numbers as correct, then that side's cause—and its interests—will seem to be right. Because the stakes can be great, stat wars can be very serious, as advocates denounce their opponents' figures while seeking to promote their own numbers.

This chapter examines some cases of recent debates over statistics. While these debates appear to be about which numbers are better, the debaters often see themselves as defending not just a statistic, but important underlying interests or principles. Stat wars can focus narrowly on the accuracy of particular numbers or on the best methods for collecting statistical data, but often they are only a small part of a long-standing dispute over some broader social issue. The cases discussed in this chapter illustrate some different types of stat wars. Reviewing these cases can help us understand both the nature of these conflicts and the ways we should respond when confronted with these dueling figures.

DEBATING A PARTICULAR NUMBER: DID ONE MILLION MEN MARCH?

In the summer of 1995, the Nation of Islam's leader, Louis Farrakan, called for African American men to join in a "Million Man March" on October 17, on the Capitol Mall in Washington, D.C. The Mall has long been a site for mobilizing huge political protests; Martin Luther King Jr. gave his "I Have a Dream" speech there in the 1963 March on Washington, and other large crowds have gathered in protest demonstrations over the war in Vietnam, abortion, women's rights, and gay and lesbian rights. Many of these gatherings inspired disputes, not only about political issues, but also about the numbers of protesters. Predictably, demonstration organizers offered big estimates for the number of people gathered; after all, a big crowd suggests both that the cause has widespread support and that the demonstration was well organized and successful. In contrast, the U.S. Park Police, who police the Mall and had been charged by Congress with making official estimates of the crowds gathered there, usually gave markedly lower estimates.[2] For example, organizers of an April 25, 1993, gay rights march on Washington estimated that more than a million demonstrators participated, but the Park Police estimated that only 300,000 attended.

It is easy to see how demonstration organizers and the Park Police could disagree. Not only do demonstration organizers have an interest in claiming that many people attended but, confronted by a huge mass of people, few organizers have any method of calculating a crowd's size. In contrast, over the years, the Park Police devised relatively sophisticated methods for estimating demonstration sizes. They used aerial photographs to reveal the portion of the Mall covered by the crowd and, since the Mall's dimensions are known, they could then calculate the area covered by people. The Park Police then multiplied the area covered by a multiplier—the estimated average number of people per square yard; the result was an estimate of the crowd's size.

The Million Man March highlighted the political nature of crowd estimates. The very name of the demonstration set a standard for its success; as the date of the march approached, its organizers insisted that the crowd would reach one million, while critics predicted that it would not. (According to the Park Police, there had been only two occasions when million-person crowds gathered on the Mall: the celebrations marking Lyndon Johnson's 1965 inauguration and the 1976 Bicentennial.) On the day of the demonstration, the organizers insisted that they had reached their goal; when Farrakan spoke, he claimed there were between a million and a half and two million people present. In contrast, the Park Police estimated the crowd's size at 400,000 (a record for civil rights demonstrations).

While the discrepancy between organizers' and the Park Police estimates fit the familiar pattern, Farrakan responded with outrage, charging that "racism, white supremacy, and the hatred of Louis Farrakan disallows them to give us credit," and threatening to sue the Park Police.[3] A team of Boston University specialists in the analysis of aerial photographs (of natural features, not crowds) examined the Park Police photographs and produced their own estimate—870,000 with a 25 percent margin of error (that is, they acknowledged that the crowd might have reached one million). The Park Police countered with more information, including additional photographs and public transportation records that showed only modestly higher traffic into central Washington on the day of the march. This led the BU researchers to revise their estimate slightly, down to 837,000.[4]

STAT WARS

Very simply, the different multipliers used to calculate the crowd's size caused the difference between the two estimates. The BU researchers assumed that the crowd was densely packed, containing six people per square meter—this is equivalent to 1.8 square feet per person, about the level of crowding in a packed elevator. It seems unlikely that a huge crowd of men would stand that close together for the hours that the rally lasted. In contrast, the Park Police assumed the crowd had about half that density, averaging 3.6 square feet per person. This is still quite densely packed for a listening audience; most crowds listening to speakers spread out and average 5.7–8.5 square feet per person.[5]

Clearly, the Million Man March attracted a very large crowd. Does it matter whether the crowd actually numbered one million, or whether it fell short of that number? In this case, the crowd's size came to represent a number of symbolic issues, including Louis Farrakan's popularity and influence among African Americans, and the degree to which the Park Police estimates reflected racism or other bias. Farrakan obviously felt committed to defending the figure of one million, and his critics delighted in insisting that the demonstration had fallen short of its goal and that Farrakan had been caught exaggerating. The BU researchers' estimate called the Park Police estimation procedures into question, although the Park Police's assumptions about crowd density seem more plausible. Still, providing crowd estimates that almost always undercut and angered demonstration organizers was a thankless task, and some of the press coverage of the BU team's estimate implied that the Park Police might have been biased. Under new instructions from Congress, the Park Police announced that they would no longer provide estimates of Mall demonstration sizes.[6]

This debate focused on an apparently simple statistical question: how many people participated in the Million Man March? There were three different answers to this question. Louis Farrakan and the march's other organizers insisted that the crowd numbered well over one million. Presumably, they derived their estimate in the same way many activists calculate the sizes of their demonstrations (and of social problems)—they guessed. The demonstration drew a huge crowd, and like other organizers of large demonstrations on the Mall, they guessed that there must have been a million people present. The second estimate, of course, came from the Park Police; they used already established methods—photographing the crowd, calculating the area it covered, and then using multiplier (one person for every 3.6 square feet) to estimate the crowd's size. The third answer, by the team from Boston University, used the same method, but applied a different multiplier (one person for every 1.8 square feet). (Obviously, it would be possible to produce any number of estimates for the crowd's size, simply by using different estimates for the crowd's density—that is, by changing the multiplier.) The issue was really very simple: How close together were the people in the crowd standing? Remarkably, although the press was interested in the debate over crowd size, reporters generally covered the story by simply reporting the competing numbers; most reporters made no effort to understand how the numbers were derived, let alone to evaluate which assumptions were more likely to produce the most accurate estimate. Instead, the press attention focused on the motivations of those making the estimates: were the Park Police biased?

The Million Man March offers a couple of important lessons. First, it is often possible to understand the basis—that is, the broad outline, if not the technical details—of statistical debates. Second, the media often do not do much to advance such understanding. Press reports often fail to explain, let alone evaluate, how different groups arrive at different numbers. Instead, media coverage is often limited to reporting that one group gives the Number X, while the other group counters with the Number Y. This gives readers and viewers little help in interpreting these different estimates.

The stakes in the debate over the Million Man March were largely symbolic. Because Farrakan had promised to bring a million men together (and because he insisted that he had done so), some commentators turned the headcount for the march into a measure of his influence or credibility. Yet, regardless of whether a million men actually showed up, it was an impressive demonstration, and the number of marchers soon became a forgotten issue. Other, more complex, debates over statistics have longer histories.

DEBATING DATA COLLECTION:
HOW SHOULD THE CENSUS COUNT PEOPLE?

The efforts to measure the Million Man March had to be completed on the day the crowd gathered—a relatively quick, inexpensive, limited operation. In contrast, consider the fantastically elaborate arrangements needed to gather the U.S. census. The U.S. Bureau of the Census has a huge budget—used to hire professional statisticians and social scientists, as well as thousands of people to collect and process the census forms, and to pay for all the equipment (not just forms, but computers, sophisticated maps, etc.) needed to conduct the census. Every ten years since 1790, the census has sought to locate and record basic information about every individual in the United States. The sheer size and complexity of this task—the U.S. population was approaching 300 million as the 2000 census approached—is astonishing. Still, the extraordinary effort that goes into preparing the census does not prevent the results from becoming controversial.

In spite of the bureau's huge budget and the professional determination of the people responsible for the census, errors are inevitable.[7] After all, hundreds of millions of people won't stand still to be counted, and confusion cannot be avoided. Some people are counted more than once; for example, college students living on campus are supposed to be counted there, but their parents sometimes also list them as living at home. But more often people go uncounted and, overall, the census undercounts the population.

In some cases, undercounting occurs because people aren't reached, perhaps because the census takers don't realize that anyone lives where they do. But, much more often, people deliberately avoid being listed in the census because they don't want to cooperate with or come to the attention of the government. Perhaps their political principles lead them to refuse to cooperate. Perhaps they are fugitives from arrest warrants or court orders. Perhaps they are undocumented aliens (illegal immigrants) who fear deportation. Perhaps they are violating welfare regulations by secretly living with (and helping to support) welfare recipients. Although other government officials (e.g., police, immigration, and welfare officials) are forbidden access to census records, many people suspect that responding to the census might get them into trouble, and they prefer to go uncounted. The resulting undercounting is not random. In general, those who go uncounted tend to be poor, urban males; this also means they are more likely to be nonwhite than the general population.

Census undercounting matters because census figures are put to use. Increasingly during the second half of the twentieth century, the federal government began using census figures to allocate major resources. Perhaps most important, the Supreme Court ruled that legislative districts needed to represent approximately equal populations. Population figures, of course, come from the census, so that a large city where a significant number of citizens went unrecorded by the census could wind up underrepresented in Congress or the state legislature. In addition, federal funds for all manner of "set-aside" programs—funds for highway construction, many social services, and so on—are allocated to the states according to their populations. Imagine a program that delivers one dollar per person to each state; for every person not counted, the state receives a dollar less than it should receive. Other people care about undercounting as well. A civil rights activist seeking to measure discrimination in employment might argue that the proportion of workers in some industry who belong to a minority group is lower than that minority's proportion in the population. But, if minority group members are undercounted in the census, the activist's calculation of the gap between the minority's share of population and their share of the jobs will be less than the actual gap.

Note that, while the census probably undercounts all groups, some groups have larger undercounts. These patterns benefit some and disadvantage others. Groups that have relatively low undercounts benefit; they receive more legislative representation, more federal funds, and so on. This gives these groups an interest in maintaining existing census procedures. In contrast, groups that have relatively more undercounting lose, and they have an interest in trying to correct the undercount.

How many people go uncounted? Obviously, no one knows exactly what this dark figure is (if we could count all the people who were not counted by the census, they could simply be added to the census total, and the problem would be solved). However, the best estimates are that the 1990 census undercounted the population by about 2 percent. At first glance, this might seem to be a relatively small percentage, but remember that even a small percentage of a large population is a fairly large number. The 1990 population was 248 million; that means that the undercount was roughly 5 million. Moreover, 2 percent is a *net* undercount (that is, after estimated overcounting is subtracted from the estimated undercount). Studies suggest that the census manages to count the vast majority of people accurately; the best estimates are that about 90 percent are properly counted, but there remain millions of errors in both overcounting and undercounting.

Moreover, undercounting is not distributed randomly throughout the population. The best estimates are that the net undercount for nonblacks was about 1.5 percent, while the net undercount for blacks was about 5 percent (there are also fairly substantial undercounts of other ethnic minorities). This means, for example, that the census significantly underestimates the size of cities and states with large minority populations.

Critics argue that the census results ought to be adjusted to reflect estimated undercounting. They recommend basing adjustments on postenumeration surveys (PES), in which specially trained census takers conduct interviews with a large sample of households. PES interviews produce more accurate data than the census forms that people are supposed to fill out and return by mail. Calculating the differences between the data gathered through the PES interviews and the census forms completed by the same households establishes a basis for estimating the undercount. (In fact, the Bureau of the Census already does PES interviewing; that is how it estimates the size of the undercount. PES analysis is the major source for the estimate that the undercount was 2 percent in 1990. Still, PES results have not been used to adjust the final census figures.)

There is fairly general agreement that the census is imperfect, that it undercounts the population, and that relatively large numbers of African Americans and other ethnic minorities are uncounted. The question is how the government ought to respond. Increasingly, demographers (including many of the professionals in the census bureau) argue that the final census results should be adjusted (that is, changed to reflect the best estimates that can be derived through PES analyses) to produce more accurate final totals. It is important to appreciate that these adjustments would change not just the total population, but the population totals for individual states, cities, and so on. Adjusting the census would probably mean, for example, that cities with large minority populations would be credited with markedly more people than the census managed to count, while mostly white, middle-class suburbs would gain relatively little over the census count. These adjusted figures would, the demographers insist, be more accurate than the inevitably flawed results of the regular census enumeration.

If the census were simply the government's best effort to collect accurate data about the population, the argument in favor of adjustment might gain wide acceptance. (Survey researchers often recalculate the results of public opinion polls in order to produce more accurate estimates by giving more weight to respondents thought to represent undersampled groups within the population.) But the census is a powerful political symbol. Every ten years, the federal government attempts to tally all Americans, and everyone is supposed to cooperate with that effort. The census is supposed to be a great compilation of individuals' responses; we do not think of it as just an estimate or a calculated guess. At least in the popular imagination, census figures represent an actual count; the very real inaccuracies in the census are not widely understood. Thus, one objection to adjusting the census findings is that many people think of census results as factual, and adjusting census figures smacks of tampering with the truth.

Remember, too, that changing the census results would be consequential. For instance, if the adjusted results for the 1990 census had been used to apportion congressional districts, two congressional seats would have shifted (Pennsylvania and Wisconsin would have each lost one, while Arizona and California would have gained one apiece). In addition, federal funding for all manner of programs would have changed; some states would have gained, but others would have lost. Choosing the basis for calculating the census is not just an abstract problem; it has real political consequences (at least so long as census figures are used as the basis for such policies as apportioning legislative districts and distributing federal funds to the states).

In recent decades, calls for adjusting the census totals have come from the mayors of big cities and other political leaders who believe they represent populations that are undercounted. Because poor nonwhites are most likely to be undercounted, and because poor nonwhites tend to vote Democratic, many of the politicians favoring adjusting the census totals have been Democrats. These politicians tend to argue that undercounting has serious consequences; they claim, for instance, that their cities and districts have lost millions of dollars in federal funding. In contrast, Republicans have tended to favor retaining the totals from the census enumeration as the official figures (and to argue that the consequences of undercounting aren't that serious). Both sides have sued in various courts, seeking to compel the use of whichever set of figures favors their interests.

The debate over the methods adopted by the census bureau is necessarily technical, and most citizens have no real grasp of how the bureau does what it does, what it might do differently, or the relative limitations of the different approaches. Those favoring adjusting the census argue that the resulting figures would be more accurate; most—although not all—social scientists favor adjustment because they are familiar with the need to weight results in survey research. Those opposed to adjusting the census warn that adjustment can never be perfect, and they question whether it makes sense to add an imperfect adjustment to an already imperfect enumeration. The courts have produced different rulings on the question but, in 1999, the U.S. Supreme Court ruled that the 2000 census could not be adjusted for purpose of congressional reapportionment. The debate will undoubtedly be renewed as planning starts for the 2010 census. Given the entrenched interests and high stakes in the outcome, the stat war over how the census counts the population is sure to continue.

STATISTICS AND CONTENTIOUS ISSUES

Both the short-lived argument over the turnout for the Million Man March and the long-standing, ongoing debate over whether the census should be adjusted are narrowly focused disputes. At issue are relatively straightforward questions—about a single number in one case and the method of measurement in the other. In contrast, many stat wars involve multifaceted debates that continue without resolution over years, even decades. Such struggles feature numerous skirmishes over different statistics related to some core social issue.

Advocates often hope to create societal consensus about some social problem, to bring a previously neglected condition to public attention, arouse concern, and promote new policies to deal with the problem. But disputes over some social issues can never reach consensus because there is real disagreement about what the problem is and what ought to be done about it. Is abortion a social problem because it involves the murder of unborn children, or is the problem that difficulty gaining access to abortion is one more way society restricts women's opportunities? Should the troubles associated with illicit drug use be resolved by decriminalizing drugs, or are even tougher laws and more vigorous enforcement the answer? Should we protect or restrict the right to bear arms?

In contrast to the debate over the turnout for the Million Man March, where the statistic became the central issue, these more complicated disputes over social issues are fundamentally disagreements over values. The abortion debate, for example, is often framed in terms of rights—the right of the fetus to societal protection vs. the right of a pregnant woman to choose abortion. Any individual's judgment that one of these rights outweighs the other derives from some interpretation of societal values. Americans value all sort of things, such as freedom and equality. While we like to imagine that our values are complementary and perfectly consistent with one another, this is a fiction: a perfectly free society is not likely to be especially egalitarian, nor is a perfectly egalitarian society likely to be especially free. Contentious social issues are contentious precisely because people make different judgments about which values are more important in the particular case: Is protecting a fetus more important than a woman's freedom to choose abortion? Does the individual's right to bear arms outweigh society's need to control violence? And so on.

Contentious issues pit competing advocates against one another. Each side is likely to have its own activists affiliated with social movement organizations (e.g., the National Right to Life Committee vs. the National Abortion and Reproductive Rights Action League). Each side can usually muster its own authorities—medical experts, religious leaders, legal scholars, social scientists, and media commentators. Depending on the issue, each side may be affiliated with a particular ideological slant (liberals vs. conservatives) or political party (Republicans vs. Democrats). Although we commonly speak of these debates as having two conflicting sides, reality is often more complex, with advocates staking out multiple positions based upon differences in their ideologies or interests. Unlike cases where there is widespread consensus about some social problem, contentious issues involve groups with competing interests making conflicting claims.

Statistics usually play a supporting role in these conflicts. The debate over abortion revolves around a clash of values, and no statistic can resolve that issue. When statistics do enter the abortion debate, advocates typically use them to show that there is broad support for their position ("Polls show that most Americans share our values or agree with us."). (Recall from chapter 2 how selective wording of questions allows advocates on both sides of the abortion and gun-control debates to point to public opinion surveys that seem to support their positions.)

Moreover, long-running debates over broad issues can lead to many different struggles over particular statistics that somehow bear on the larger topic.

Consider issues of equality. Americans readily endorse equality as a value, yet inequalities of race, gender, and class have been—and continue to be—visible and important. American history features lengthy, ongoing campaigns by the civil rights movement, the women's movement, the labor movement, and other advocates claiming that particular kinds of people are blocked from full equality. Typically, these (usually liberal) advocates insist that, whatever progress may have been made, serious inequities remain, and these warrant making further significant changes in social policy to foster equality (examples might include raising the minimum wage, establishing tougher antidiscrimination policies, and so on). In contrast, their (usually conservative) opponents argue that considerable social progress toward equality already has been achieved (implying that additional drastic changes in social policies are not only not needed, but may cause harm by unnecessarily restricting people's freedom).

Arguments about recent changes in the distribution of income are just one small aspect of this larger debate over equality.[8] Many Americans like to imagine that their economy fosters growing prosperity. This vision finds statistical support in measures of per capita personal income (basically the nation's total income divided by its population). Per capita income rose fairly steadily in the second half of the twentieth century (see the first column in Table 6). Those with a stake in defending the status

Table 6. *Gross Domestic Product Per Capita
and Average Hourly Earnings, 1959–1999*

Year	Per Capita Income[a]	Hourly Earnings[b]
1959	$12,985	$6.69
1964	14,707	7.33
1969	17,477	7.98
1974	18,989	8.28
1979	21,635	8.17
1984	23,171	7.80
1989	26,552	7.64
1994	28,156	7.40
1999	32,439	7.86

[a] Gross domestic product per capita in 1996 dollars.

[b] Average hourly wages in private nonagricultural industries in 1982 dollars.

SOURCE: U.S. Department of Commerce, *Economic Report of the President 2000* (Washington, D.C., 2000), pp. 341, 360.

quo (not just conservatives, but political incumbents generally) can point to the growth in per capita income as proof that things have been getting better ("Prosperity is increasing! There's more money per person. There's no need to change.").

In response, critics of the status quo (often liberals, but also the incumbents' challengers) cite statistics showing that the economy is not getting better—and may actually be getting worse. For example, average hourly earnings peaked in the early

1970s and generally fell during the century's last three decades (see the second column in Table 6). Of course, this seems troubling ("Things are getting worse! People are earning less per hour of work. We need to do something.").

How is it possible for the average income per person to rise at the same time the average hourly wage fell? Changes in the workforce help account for this apparent discrepancy. Most important, the proportion of the population in the workforce grew, in particular, the proportion of employed women rose. (As a growing percentage of families featured two wage-earners, average family incomes rose. If, on average, the husband's income declined a bit, this was offset by increases in the wife's income as she entered the workforce or increased her hours.) If a growing proportion of the population is employed, per capita income can grow, even if hourly wages decline somewhat. (Increases in the number of hours individuals work can have the same effect.)

Defenders of the status quo argue that hourly earnings are a poor measure of economic prosperity. They note, for example, that real hourly compensation (that is, wages plus the value of benefits) generally rose in recent decades. Moreover, year-to-year comparisons of income must be converted to constant dollars to adjust for inflation, and the status quo's defenders claim that the Consumer Price Index (CPI) used to make the adjustments for inflation exaggerates the amount of inflation (and thereby underestimates the growth in the value of wages). By correcting the CPI and taking the value of benefits into account, these advocates can make a case that hourly compensation in fact rose in recent decades.

Their critics' response to this rosy view focuses on income inequality. The old aphorism "The rich get richer and the poor get poorer" expresses this critique. Contemporary critics warn about the "shrinking middle class." There is a great deal of evidence that income inequality has grown in recent decades. Whether we consider family incomes or individual incomes (and whether we look at the incomes of males or females, of black or white workers), the same pattern emerges: incomes among those already earning more have been growing faster than the incomes of those earning less. Typically, these measures reveal that the incomes of those earning the least (say, the lowest-earning fifth of the population) actually declined during the same period that the incomes of those earning the most (the highest-earning fifth of the population) showed substantial increases. In effect, the rich *have* been getting richer, and the poor poorer.

It is important to appreciate that these measures of growing inequality usually do not track particular individuals through time. That is, when we compare, say, the poorest fifth of the population in Year 1 with the poorest fifth ten years later, we are not necessarily talking about the same people; some poor people experience upward mobility. Even if incomes in the lowest-earning fifth of the population fell between Year 1 and Year 10, an individual who was in the lowest fifth in Year 1 may, in Year 10, be in some higher-earning category (for an extreme example, imagine someone working at a mininum-wage job in Year 1 while going to law school; in Year 10, the same individual might be a highly paid lawyer who falls into the highest-earning fifth). Such upwardly mobile people create vacancies in the lowest-earning fifth, and some of those slots will be filled by newcomers just entering the workforce. On the other hand, while upward mobility does occur, it is far from universal; many people—particularly those with limited education and job skills—remain trapped in the lowest-earning fifth and experience declining incomes. While some individuals may not notice the growing inequality in the larger society because they personally experience upward mobility, others find themselves falling further behind.

The debate over income distribution is complex. The government produces vast amounts of economic data, and economists disagree about the best measures (the dispute over the most reasonable way to calculate the CPI is only one example). By choosing carefully among the available statistics, advocates can find support for very different positions ("Rising per capita income shows growing prosperity!" "No, falling hourly income shows diminishing prosperity!"). In the resulting barrage of statistics, proponents of different positions argue that their numbers are significant, while their opponents' figures are poor measures of whatever is at issue.

Making sense of this confusion is challenging. Clearly, it is better to evaluate competing statistical claims, rather than listening to only one side, and it helps to understand as much as possible about what the different numbers mean. It also helps to realize how social changes affect statistics and their significance: more women are working and people are having fewer children (two changes that lead to higher family and per capita incomes); a growing proportion of jobs are highly skilled (which contributes to income inequality); and so on. There is, alas, no single, authoritative measure of prosperity and, as society changes, various statistics may become better or worse indicators of economic and social conditions.

Debates over topics as broad as equality have countless facets; although this discussion has focused on income inequality, we might have chosen to focus on inequalities of race, gender, and so on. The broader issue is grounded in philosophical disputes over the nature of not just equality, but also liberty, justice, and other values, and over how government and other institutions should devise social policies to foster and protect those values. With a broad, mutifaceted issue, virtually every facet— income inequality, public opinion, criminal justice, quality of health care, access to employment and higher education, and on and on—can be contested, and in each of these contests advocates can cite statistics to support different points of view.[9]

Whenever there is disagreement about the statistical evidence, it is possible to look more closely, to discover how different measurement choices, different definitions, or other factors can explain the disparities. But, of course, this can be a lot of work; few people will make the effort to examine original sources in order to reconcile a stat war. And, even when it is possible to clarify a specific statistical disagreement, that clarification will not resolve the larger debate about the broader social issue. Again, debates over broad social issues have their roots in competing interests and different values. While advocates for different positions tend to invoke statistics as evidence to bolster their arguments, statistics in and of themselves cannot resolve these debates.

Still, our society makes it easy to create and spread statistics about social problems. This is important because we often equate numbers with "facts." Treating a number as a fact implies that it is indisputable. It should be no suprise, then, when people interested in some social problem collect relevant statistics and present them as facts. This is a way for them to claim authority, to argue that the facts ("It's true!") support their position.

One interesting way of claiming authority in recent years has been to publish collections of social problems statistics in small, specialized reference books. The titles of these volumes often emphasize the factual nature of the contents, even though the books frequently promote a particular ideology or the interests of a specific group. Compare two books: William J. Bennett, the conservative politician, published *The Index of Leading Cultural Indicators: American Society at the End of the Twentieth Century*, while social scientists Marc Miringoff and Marque-Luisa Miringoff wrote *The Social Health of the Nation: How America Is Really Doing*.[10] Both books present multiple social statistics intended to document trends over the past two or three decades. Both books insist that these trends are troubling. According to Bennett: "In two generations, America has undergone dramatic and traumatic social change—the kind that one would normally associate with cataclysmic natural [*sic*] events like famine, revolution, or war. Civilizations stand on precious few pillars, and during the last three and a half decades, many of ours have fractured."[11] Similarly, Miringoff and Miringoff argue: "On the whole, long-term trends in social performance may be viewed as less than encouraging. While some indicators show improvement . . . , many have worsened significantly over time. . . . These are warning signs which require attention."[12]

Attempts to track social indicators over time confront many of the problems discussed in earlier chapters. These include the basic difficulties in defining and measuring social conditions. However, there is a larger problem: the government does not collect and publish many series of statistics for social indicators. This is in sharp contrast to the government's treatment of economic statistics; anyone who follows the news cannot help but hear regular (usually monthly) statistical updates about the balance of trade, consumer confidence, the Consumer Price Index, housing starts, unemployment, and so on. Many of these measures have been collected and published for decades. In contrast, there are few comparable indexes of social trends, they tend to be published less frequently (often annually), and the lag time between data collection and publication tends to be longer.[13] In addition, with the exception of population statistics and crime rates, relatively few data have been collected at regular intervals, using standard measures, for enough years to establish clear trends.

Moreover, social statistics pose problems of interpretation. Even when data are available, they do not speak for themselves. For example, both Bennett and Miringoff and Miringoff note the increase in child poverty. From 1970 to 1996, the percentage of children (under age 18) living in poverty rose, from 14.9 percent in 1970, to 19.8 percent in 1996. (In contrast, the percentage of

Americans aged 65 and above living in poverty fell markedly during the same period, from 24.6 percent in 1970, to 10.8 percent in 1996. That is, in 1970 children were much less likely to be poor than were older Americans, but in 1996 the positions had been reversed.) What should we make of this shift? Miringoff and Miringoff note that the U.S. rate of child poverty is far higher than those found in other industrialized nations, although they point out that other countries "have relatively high child poverty rates before the application of tax and transfer programs designed to improve the status of children."[14] In contrast, Bennett's interpretation of the data locates the cause of child poverty in family structure: "Poverty afflicts nearly one of every two mother-only families (45 percent in 1992) and fewer than one in ten married-couple families (8 percent in 1992)"; and "Almost 60 percent of children under 6 living in families with only a mother had an income below the poverty level, more than five times as many as children under 6 in married-couple families (10.6 percent)."[15]

How should we interpret rising child poverty? For Bennett, a political and social conservative, child poverty is a "cultural indicator," a product of a deteriorating culture that tolerates out-of-wedlock births, divorce, and children raised in single-parent families. That is, cultural changes have led to more children in single-parent families, which in turn means more children live in poverty. Presumably, Bennet would argue that the ultimate solution for child poverty would be a return to traditional values or virtues that would ensure that children are raised in intact families. In contrast, Miringoff and Miringoff do not specify the

causes of rising child poverty, but they clearly favor social policies to provide additional support for poor children. A reader
might infer that they locate the causes of child poverty in the sort
of structural inequalities emphasized in liberal analyses, rather
than in the cultural failures decried by conservatives.

This example reveals that facts do not speak for themselves.
The previous section used a stat war about income inequality to
illustrate how debaters choose to measure social problems in
different ways. But the competing interpretations of the growing
percentage of poor children involve a single method of measurement, a relatively clear-cut social indicator (children living in
households below the poverty level), and high-quality data collected by a federal agency; yet advocates interpret the *same*
numbers very differently. Where Bennett finds evidence of moral
collapse, Miringoff and Miringoff see inadequate social policies
to protect children's welfare. We may think of statistics as facts,
but people make facts meaningful, and analysts' ideologies
shape the meanings they assign to social statistics.

Worse, these reference books' efforts to claim statistical
authority do not always involve high-quality data. Earlier chapters have noted the relative ease with which statistics circulate,
even numbers based on guesses, peculiar definitions, deceptive
measures, and weak samples, to say nothing of numbers that
have been mangled to produce mutant statistics. Bad numbers
may originate in particular—even glaring—errors, but they can
live on indefinitely in media reports. Reference books compile
statistics—good and bad—and reprint them without subjecting
them to much critical analysis. For example, the Women's Action

Coalition (WAC) published *WAC Stats: The Facts about Women.*
This book repeats some flawed statistics discussed in earlier
chapters (e.g., "150,000 American women die of anorexia a year";
"Gay and lesbian teenagers are up to 3 times more likely to commit suicide than their heterosexual peers.") among the hundreds
of statistical claims in its pages.[16] The source for each claim is
given in a footnote, and the range of sources is extraordinary:
some numbers come from government documents, but others
come from flyers, handouts, or fact sheets distributed by
activists; and most seem to have been taken from newspaper or
newsmagazine stories. That is, this reference book depends
upon what historians would call secondary, rather than primary,
sources. For example, if a sociologist conducts a study and pub-
lishes the results in a scholarly journal, that is a primary source;
but a newspaper story referring to the study's findings is at least
an additional step removed from the research—it is a secondary
source. In most cases, the newspaper story gives little or no
information about the key decisions that shape research results
(how concepts were defined and measured, what the sample
was, and so on). Worse, the press often fails to differentiate
between statistics produced through carefully designed research
and far less reliable numbers. Newspaper readers have enough
trouble evaluating the statistics they find in newspaper stories.
When a reference book uncritically copies hundreds of such
numbers from newspaper stories and other, even less reliable
sources, and presents them as straightforward facts, it makes an
unjustified claim to statistical authority. And, because many of
these reference books are intended to present data that support

particular ideologies or interests, they make no effort to include competing statistical claims that might lead their readers to be cautious. Just because someone claims authority does not mean we ought to grant it.

INTERPRETING STAT WARS

Advocates use statistics to support their claims about social problems. Rarely will they invoke numbers that seem to call their claims into question. So long as they can mobilize consensus about a social problem, so long as their claims encounter little opposition, advocates' numbers go unquestioned. In contrast, debates over social issues feature competing, contradictory claims that often include arguments over statistics—what I have called stat wars.

Stat wars create confusion. Because we tend to think of numbers as facts, most of us have difficulty reconciling conflicting figures. Certainly stat wars often distress the press. Ideally, press coverage presents the facts, and reporters and editors like to repeat statistics because numbers seem factual.[17] When the press is confronted with what are clearly contradictory numbers (as in the case of the conflicting estimates for the size of the Million Man March), it has trouble doing more than simply acknowledging the disagreement. Even advocates find stat wars troubling. Advocates often believe their own statistics, and they respond to challenges to their numbers with outrage: at best, their opponents are misinformed; at worst, the competing figures are outright lies.

While some social problems statistics are deliberate deceptions, many—probably the great majority—of bad statistics are the result of confusion, incompetence, innumeracy, or selective, self-righteous efforts to produce numbers that reaffirm principles and interests that their advocates consider just and right. The best response to stat wars is not to try and guess who's lying or, worse, simply to assume that the people we disagree with are the ones telling lies. Rather, we need to watch for the standard causes of bad statistics—guessing, questionable definitions or methods, mutant numbers, and inappropriate comparisons. In some cases, we may conclude that one number is right and another is deeply flawed; in others, we may discover that the different figures reflect people choosing different methods to answer different questions. Whatever we conclude, we should come away with a better understanding of all the statistics.

6

THINKING ABOUT SOCIAL STATISTICS

The Critical Approach

There are cultures in which people believe that some objects have magical powers; anthropologists call these objects fetishes. In our society, statistics are a sort of fetish. We tend to regard statistics as though they are magical, as though they are more than mere numbers. We treat them as powerful representations of the truth; we act as though they distill the complexity and confusion of reality into simple facts. We use statistics to convert complicated social problems into more easily understood estimates, percentages, and rates. Statistics direct our concern; they show us what we ought to worry about and how much we ought to worry. In a sense, the social problem becomes the statistic and, because we treat statistics as true and incontrovertible, they achieve a kind of fetishlike, magical control over how we view social problems. We think of statistics as facts that we discover, not as numbers we create.

But, of course, statistics do not exist independently; people have to create them. Reality is complicated, and every statistic is someone's summary, a simplification of that complexity. Every statistic must be created, and the process of creation always involves choices that affect the resulting number and therefore affect what we understand after the figures summarize and simplify the problem. People who create statistics must choose definitions—they must define what it is they want to count— and they must choose their methods—the ways they will go about their counting. Those choices shape every good statistic, and every bad one. Bad statistics simplify reality in ways that distort our understanding, while good statistics minimize that distortion. No statistic is perfect, but some are less imperfect than others. Good or bad, every statistic reflects its creators' choices.

This book offers some guidelines for thinking critically about social statistics. It identifies some common problems with social statistics and illustrates them with specific examples. It is often easier to understand a particular example than to understand and recognize the general problem or principle that the example illustrates. Still, I hope that, having read this book, you have become more familiar with some of the most common flaws that bedevil social statistics: that you can ask some basic questions about a statistic's origins (definition, measurement, sampling, and the other issues covered in chapter 2); that you are familiar with some of the ways statistics can be mangled (chapter 3); that you understand the risks of inappropriate comparisons (chapter 4); and that you can do more than simply throw up your hands when confronted with a debate featuring competing statistics (chapter 5). But a short book like this one cannot hope to offer a comprehensive list of statistical errors.

In order to interpret statistics, we need more than a checklist of common errors. We need a general approach, an orientation, a mind-set that we can use to think about new statistics that we encounter. We ought to approach statistics thoughtfully. This can be hard to do, precisely because so many people in our society treat statistics as fetishes. We might call this the mind-set of the Awestruck—the people who don't think critically, who act as though statistics have magical powers. The Awestruck know they don't always understand the statistics they hear, but this doesn't bother them. After all, who can expect to understand magical numbers? The reverential fatalism of the Awestruck is not thoughtful—it is a way of avoiding thought. We need a different approach. Three come to mind; they are the mind-sets of the Naive, the Cynical, and the Critical.

THE NAIVE

The Naive are slightly more sophisticated than the Awestruck. Many people believe they understand a bit about statistics—they know something about percentages, rates, and the like—but their approach is basically accepting. They presume that statistics are generally accurate, that they mean what they seem to mean. The Naive are often at least somewhat innumerate; they occasionally may be confused by basic mathematical ideas ("A million, a billion—what's the difference? They're all big numbers."). And, as the name suggests, the Naive tend to be innocent and trusting; they don't question numbers or wonder how those numbers might be shaped by interests of the people behind them. The Naive are sincere, and they assume that the people who present statistics are equally sincere, and that their numbers are valid.

The Naive are not just consumers of others' numbers; they also can create and disseminate statistics. When activists offer estimates for the scope of some social problem, their attitude is often one of naïveté ("It's a big problem, and this is a big number—it must be about right."). And, once a number is in circulation, Naive reporters may be willing to repeat it and pass it along ("This is the only number out there, so it must be pretty accurate."). When they are innumerate, the Naive often generate mutant statistics; when they try to repeat figures they don't completely understand, it is easy for them to produce new, mangled numbers.

In addition to creating, spreading, and mangling statistics, the Naive (and their slightly less critical cousins, the Awestruck) probably account for the vast majority of the audience that hears these numbers. The Naive are unlikely to question numbers—not even the most implausible exaggerations; after all, the Naive usually don't suspect statistics might be bad, and even if they do, they have no good ways of detecting bad statistics. They are unlikely to wonder about definitions or measurements, or to spot inappropriate comparisons, and they find debates over statistics completely bewildering. The Naive form a wonderfully receptive audience ("They say 150,000 young women die from anorexia each year! That's terrible!"), easily influenced and not at all critical. At the same time, the Naive assign no special value to statistics; they may be equally influenced by a disturbing example, an acquaintance's opinion, a rumor, or other sources of information. The Naive not only fail to suspect that bad statistics have flaws, but they often do not recognize when statistics are pretty good. The great majority of the audience for social statistics is, at least to some degree, Naive.

THE CYNICAL

Fewer people can be described as Cynical, but they are extremely important. The Cynical are suspicious of statistics; they are convinced that numbers are probably flawed, and that those flaws are probably intentional. They view statistics as efforts to manipulate—they are worse than "damned lies." They don't trust numbers ("You can prove anything with statistics.").

The Cynical are most important as originators of statistics. People who create statistics often have an agenda—to promote their industry, their cause, their ideology, their group—and they view statistics as a means of furthering that end. The Cynical design research that will produce the results they want: they word questions so as to encourage particular responses; they choose samples likely to respond the way they want; they massage the data until the results take the form they desire; in extreme instances, they simply lie and make up whatever numbers suit their purposes. The Cynical count on their audience being mostly Naive; the Naive will accept whatever numbers they're given, so why not give them whatever numbers will influence them to think or do whatever the Cynical want?

The distinction between the Cynical and the Naive is not as sharp as it first seems. Many people who promote statistics want to persuade; they have interests and agendas to promote, and they see statistics as a tool toward that end. These qualities might seem to place them among the Cynical. Yet, at the same time, these people often have an imperfect understanding of the limitations of the numbers they are promoting—the Cynical are not immune to innumeracy. This means that they also are, in a sense, Naive, and may believe whatever their own figures seem to show.

Another role the Cynical play is as members of the audience for statistics. Here they suspect there must be something wrong with whatever numbers they hear. Because the Cynical suspect that "you can prove anything with statistics," they can justify ignoring all numbers—particularly those that challenge their beliefs. This sort of cynicism is most obvious in debates over contentious social issues, such as abortion or gun control. The Cynical allied with one side on an issue are quick to discount any statistics offered by the other side. They may be surprisingly sophisticated when pointing out the flaws in numbers they don't like, although they rarely examine their own side's figures with the same critical eye. And, of course, their cynical discounting of statistics and the people who use them further confuses the Naive.

It is important to be clear: this book is not intended to swell the ranks of the Cynical; I do not want to encourage you to discount every statistic as worthless. We need not choose between remaining among the Naive or joining the Cynical. There is a third, far superior option.

THE CRITICAL

This third choice is to approach statistics critically. Being critical does not mean being negative or hostile—it is not cynicism. The Critical approach statistics thoughtfully; they avoid the extremes of both naive acceptance and cynical rejection of the numbers they encounter. Instead, the Critical attempt to evaluate numbers, to distinguish between good statistics and bad statistics.

The Critical understand that, while some social statistics may be pretty good, they are never perfect. Every statistic is a way of summarizing complex information into relatively simple numbers. Inevitably, some information, some of the complexity, is lost whenever we use statistics. The Critical recognize that this is an inevitable limitation of statistics. Moreover, they realize that every statistic is the product of choices—the choice between defining a category broadly or narrowly, the choice of one measurement over another, the choice of a sample. People choose definitions, measurements, and samples for all sorts of reasons: perhaps they want to emphasize some aspect of a problem; perhaps it is easier or cheaper to gather data in a particular way— many considerations can come into play. Every statistic is a compromise among choices. This means that every definition—and every measurement and every sample—probably has limitations and can be criticized.

Being Critical means more than simply pointing to the flaws in a statistic. Again, every statistic has flaws. The issue is whether a particular statistic's flaws are severe enough to damage its usefulness. Is the definition so broad that it encompasses too many false positives (or so narrow that it excludes too many false negatives)? How would changing the definition alter the statistic? Similarly, how do the choices of measurements and samples affect the statistic? What would happen if different measures or samples were chosen? And how is the statistic used? Is it being interpreted appropriately, or has its meaning been mangled to create a mutant statistic? Are the comparisons that are being made appropriate, or are apples being confused with oranges? How do different choices produce the conflicting numbers found in stat wars? These are the sorts of questions the Critical ask.

CONFRONTING THE INEVITABLE

As a practical matter, it is virtually impossible for citizens in contemporary society to avoid statistics about social problems. Statistics arise in all sorts of ways, and in almost every case the people promoting statistics want to persuade us. Activists use statistics to convince us that social problems are serious and deserve our attention and concern. Charities use statistics to encourage donations. Politicians use statistics to persuade us that they understand society's problems and that they deserve our support. The media use statistics to make their reporting more dramatic, more convincing, more compelling. Corporations use statistics to promote their products and improve their profits. Researchers use statistics to document their findings and support their conclusions. Those with whom we agree use statistics to reassure us that we're on the right side, while our opponents use statistics to try and convince us that we are wrong. Statistics are one of the standard types of evidence used by people in our society.

It is not possible simply to ignore statistics, to pretend they don't exist. That sort of head-in-the-sand approach would be too costly. Without statistics, we limit our ability to think thoughtfully about our society; without statistics, we have no accurate ways of judging how big a problem may be, whether it is getting worse, or how well the policies designed to address that problem actually work. And Awestruck or Naive attitudes toward statistics are no better than ignoring statistics; statistics have no magical properties, and it is foolish to assume that all statistics are equally valid. Nor is a Cynical approach the answer; statistics are too widespread and too useful to be automatically discounted.

It would be nice to have a checklist, a set of items we could consider in evaluating any statistic. One could think of the topics discussed in this book as an outline for such a checklist: the list might detail potential problems with definitions, measurements, sampling, mutation, and so on. These are in fact common sorts of flaws found in many statistics, but they should not be considered a formal, complete checklist. It is probably impossible to produce a complete list of statistical flaws—no matter how long the list, there will be other possible problems that could affect statistics.

The goal is not to memorize a list, but to develop a thoughtful approach. Becoming Critical about statistics requires being prepared to ask questions about numbers. When encountering a new statistic in, say, a news report, the Critical try to assess it. What might be the sources for this number? How could one go about producing the figure? Who produced the number, and what interests might they have? What are the different ways key terms might have been defined, and which definitions have been chosen? How might the phenomena be measured, and which measurement choices have been made? What sort of sample was gathered, and how might that sample affect the result? Is the statistic being properly interpreted? Are comparisons being made, and if so, are the comparisons appropriate? Are there competing statistics? If so, what stakes do the opponents have in the issue, and how are those stakes likely to affect their use of statistics? And is it possible to figure out why the statistics seem to disagree, what the differences are in the ways the competing sides are using figures?

At first, this list of questions may seem overwhelming. How can an ordinary person—someone who reads a statistic in a magazine article or hears it on a news broadcast—determine the answers to such questions? Certainly news reports rarely give detailed information on the processes by which statistics are created. And few of us have time to drop everything and investigate the background of some new number we encounter. Being Critical, it seems, involves an impossible amount of work.

In practice, however, the Critical need not investigate the origin of every statistic. Rather, being Critical means appreciating the inevitable limitations that affect all statistics, rather than being Awestruck in the presence of numbers. It means not being too credulous, not accepting every statistic at face value (as the Naive do). But it also means appreciating that statistics, while always imperfect, can be useful. Instead of automatically discounting every statistic (in the fashion of the Cynical), the Critical reserve judgment. When confronted with an interesting number, they may try to learn more, to evaluate, to weigh the figure's strengths and weaknesses.

Of course, this Critical approach need not—and should not—be limited to statistics. It ought to apply to all the evidence we encounter when we scan a news report, or listen to a speech, whenever we learn about social problems. Claims about social problems often feature dramatic, compelling examples; the Critical might ask whether an example is likely to be a typical case or an extreme, exceptional instance. Claims about social problems often include quotations from different sources, and the Critical might wonder why those sources have spoken and why they have been quoted: Do they have particular expertise? Do they stand to benefit if they influence others? Claims about social problems usually involve arguments about the problem's causes and potential solutions. The Critical might ask whether these arguments are convincing. Are they logical? Does the proposed solution seem feasible and appropriate? And so on. Being Critical—adopting a skeptical, analytical stance when confronted with claims—is an approach that goes far beyond simply dealing with statistics.

Statistics are not magical. Nor are they always true—or always false. Nor need they be incomprehensible. Adopting a Critical approach offers an effective way of responding to the numbers we are sure to encounter. Being Critical requires more thought, but failing to adopt a Critical mind-set makes us powerless to evaluate what others tell us. When we fail to think critically, the statistics we hear might just as well be magical.

Afterword

BAD STATISTICS: WHAT'S THE PROBLEM?

In the spring of 2011, almost exactly ten years after this book first appeared, Arizona Republican Senator Jon Kyl, speaking on the Senate floor, declared: "If you want an abortion, you go to Planned Parenthood, and that's well over 90 percent of what Planned Parenthood does." Anticipating that this sound bite was likely to became fodder for late-night comedians and fact-checking websites, the senator's office quickly distributed a statement explaining that the remark "was not intended to be a factual statement but rather to illustrate that Planned Parenthood . . . does subsidize abortions." This clarification, in turn, attracted further derisive commentary about the suggestion that a statistical claim need not be "a factual statement."[1]

These two quotations reveal a good deal about the place of statistics in our discussions of the public issues that continue to plague us in the new century. We are, on the one hand, eager to invoke numbers, because they seem to add authority to our claims. We like to imagine that numbers are facts, and someone who uses a number is understood to be stating a fact. To say that abortions are "well over 90 percent of what Planned Parenthood does," is to invite one's listeners to assume that somebody somehow measured what Planned Parenthood does, and found that abortion accounted for the vast majority of that activity.

Of course Kyl's claim that abortions account for most of what Planned Parenthood does was clearly false. Most people realize that Planned Parenthood offers a range of contraceptive and other reproductive health services; they know enough about the organization to be pretty sure that the senator's 90 percent figure could not be factual. Still, reasonable people might disagree about the correct figure. Planned Parenthood's own materials indicate that their organization provided about 11 million services in 2010, including some 329,000 abortions; that might suggest that abortions represent only about 3 percent of "what Planned Parenthood does."[2] However, many clients receive multiple services during a single visit to Planned Parenthood; those 11 million services were provided to "nearly 3 million people," so if we ask what percentage of the people who come to Planned Parenthood receive an abortion, the answer is something over 10 percent (329,000/nearly 3,000,000). That's more than 3 percent, but still a whole lot less than "well over 90 percent." (Another way to think about this is that, based on the most recent statistics, Planned Parenthood provides roughly a quarter of the nation's abortions.[3])

But it was Senator Kyl's office's clarification—that the claim about "well over 90 percent" "was not intended to be a factual statement"—that makes this a particularly wonderful example. That clarification inspired its own round of comedic commentary. But why? We assume that politicians will commit rhetorical excesses, that they will exaggerate their own virtues and their opponents' flaws. If the senator had characterized Planned Parenthood as, say, a major abortion provider, no one would have blinked. But assigning a number—particularly an obviously incorrect number—crosses some boundary of permissible rhetorical license. Numbers imply that a claim is factual. Citing an obviously incorrect number makes one seem ignorant, foolish, silly, even dishonest. And backpedaling to say that the obviously incorrect number "was not intended to be a factual statement," only makes things worse, by suggesting that one doesn't know—or doesn't see the need to play by—the rules for acceptable rhetoric.

In our world, knowingly misusing numbers is scandalous. We encounter frequent exposés—news stories about police forces doctoring their arrest records to make their cities' crime rates seem lower, teachers and principals rigging their students' standardized test scores to boost their schools' rankings, financial rating services giving good ratings to risky investments in order to keep the business of the firms sponsoring those investments, corporations juggling their books so as to meet their projected quarterly profits and thereby retain investors' confidence, and so on.[4] In each of these cases, a revelation that people have knowingly produced inaccurate figures is likely to lead to a scandal.

Why is it scandalous? Because we depend on statistics. We

cannot understand the complexities of our world without counting and measuring. Statistics have become a vital tool for keeping track of what's happening, and we depend upon their accuracy. So when people—regardless of whether they are cops or
accountants or senators—start monkeying with numbers, they
threaten our confidence in our social institutions. We are scan-
dalized.

At the same time, many of us are leery of the numbers that
surround us. We both depend on the accuracy of statistics that
inform our thinking, and worry that those figures may not be
reliable. Publishing this book brought me into contact with all
sorts of people, including journalists, judges, activists, and legislators. Virtually all of them agreed with my thesis, that people
need to think more critically about statistics. Of course, many
other people have been making similar arguments for a very long
time; there is even a movement among educators to advance the
cause of statistical literacy (a.k.a. quantitative literacy, numeracy, etc.).[5]

In my experience, pretty much everyone agrees that people
should apply critical standards to the numbers they encounter in
the news. So why doesn't the problem go away? Numbers that
seem debatable, dubious, even downright ludicrous abound.

My favorite recent example also comes from the spring of
2011; it is a blog post declaring that California has "roughly 37 million deaths from smoking-related issues per year."[6] The blogger
managed to conflate California's total population (37 million in
2010), with the state's number of smoking-related deaths, producing a sentence that implies that smoking kills California's

entire population—every year, no less. On the one hand, I can understand how someone might make this mistake: antismoking advocates think that smoking is a big problem, and 37 million is a big number—so, they might tell themselves, it's probably about right. But is it unreasonable to expect even smoking's most dedicated opponents to pause and think, "Thirty-seven million? That's an awful lot—I wonder if that's right." And it is an awfully big number; the total annual number of deaths worldwide, from all causes, is about 58 million. If California had 37 million smoking-related deaths, those deaths would account for two-thirds of the world's fatalities. The actual annual figure for smoking-related deaths in California is probably closer to 37 thousand than to 37 million.

Why do bad statistics continue to befuddle us? Why is this an ongoing problem?

There are various answers to this question. One of the most popular comes from those we might call the culture warriors They say, "It's the other guys' fault." Culture warriors hold competing viewpoints for thinking about society—different ideologies—and they define themselves not only in terms of which beliefs they hold dear, but also in terms of which ideas they oppose. Twenty-five years ago, it was common for intellectuals to complain that the news media presented a homogenized, taken-for-granted worldview. Today, thanks especially to the expansion of cable television and the emergence of the Internet, we live in what I think of as a *Crossfire* culture (named for the early CNN program where a liberal and a conservative railed against each other about the issues of the day). But *Crossfire* occupied a single slot in CNN's schedule; it was the lone show on that network that presented debate as entertainment. Today, we have entire cable-news networks dedicated to crossfiring, with Fox News and MSNBC framing the news in conservative and liberal terms, respectively, and regularly denouncing the coverage on the rival network.

In the partisan arenas of cable news and the blogosphere, statistics that seem to reaffirm the correctness of one's own position are welcomed, but those that challenge that position must be disputed. Senator Kyl's claim that abortions are "well over 90 percent of what Planned Parenthood does" occurred during a political debate; he was speaking in response to a liberal opponent's argument that Planned Parenthood provided vital services. His assertion inspired Internet commentary that included claims from liberal defenders of Planned Parenthood who implied that the senator's bad number was just one more example of conservatives playing fast and loose with facts, but also counterclaims from conservatives insisting that liberals' criticism of the senator's statistic was a red herring, an unimportant distraction intended to divert attention from the real issue—that Planned Parenthood is a major abortion provider.[7]

Culture warriors tend to be remarkably adept at spotting the bad statistics in their opponents' arguments. For them, dubious figures stand as proof of their opponents' inclinations toward perfidy and chicanery. However, the critical thinking skills that are exercised in disputing the other guys' numbers seem to vanish when culture warriors are confronted with statistics that support their own positions. Maybe our numbers aren't exactly right, they concede, but that hardly matters. Thus, Planned Parenthood's supporters made fun of the senator's ridiculous estimate, even as their opponents defended the underlying critique of Planned Parenthood.

We need to recognize that both liberals and conservatives, as well as adherents to all sorts of other ideologies, regularly try to demolish the other guys' statistics, even as they insist that their own numbers aren't all that bad. This means that, however much we might like to think that it is only those other guys who misuse numbers, no side has a monopoly on bad stats. Only the truest believers can contend that all dubious data come from their ideological opponents.

Well, if ideology isn't the explanation, what causes all those flawed numbers? Another explanation comes from numeracy's advocates, those folks calling for improving quantitative literacy.[8] They argue that bad statistics flourish because people are innumerate, the mathematical equivalent of illiterate. Just as literacy's advocates worry that too many people leave school with inadequate reading skills and call for renewed emphasis on reading instruction, numeracy's advocates point to people's inadequate math skills and urge upgrading how math is taught. Not surprisingly, a large share of numeracy advocates are educators, often teachers or professors of mathematics, or education school faculty who specialize in mathematics education; others come from other disciplines, such as economics or geology, but tend to teach courses in statistics or quantitative methods. All of these educators encounter students who seem to have trouble thinking mathematically, students who have not learned math skills they need. Surely, they argue, math instruction needs to be improved.

I don't oppose upgrading mathematics education, but I'm not sure that it will do much to reduce the flood of bad statistics. Take our two examples. Senator Kyl's claim that abortions are "well over 90 percent of what Planned Parenthood does" was not a result of some erroneous calculation. Rather, the problem arose when a politician created an off-the-cuff—and obviously implausible—statistic to make a point. If he had said that Planned Parenthood provides a lot of abortions, no one would have disputed the claim. "Well over 90 percent" is certainly "a lot," but "a lot" often means much less than "well over 90 percent," and it is not clear to me that this distinction is at bottom mathematical.

Similarly, when we read that California has "roughly 37 million deaths from smoking-related issues per year," it takes only a moment to suspect that that statistic must be ridiculous. Even if we concede that smoking kills a lot of Californians, 37 million is a *whole* lot, way more than any conceivable death toll among the state's smokers. Again, is this primarily a failure in mathematics instruction? I don't think so.

And let me add a third example: baseball statistics. People—lots and lots of people—talk quite comfortably about players' batting averages. A batting average is the proportion of official at-bats that result in a hit; if a batter's appearance at the plate ends in a walk, being hit by a pitch, or a sacrifice, it does not count as an official at-bat, and is not included in calculating the player's batting average. Similarly, the earned run average is one of the most common measures of a baseball pitcher's performance. It is calculated by taking the number of runs scored by batters the pitcher faced (minus runs scored due to errors), dividing it by the number of innings pitched, and then multiplying the result by nine (because there are nine innings in a complete game). Understanding either of these statistics requires knowing what counts (strike-outs count—but walks don't—when calculating a batting average, just as runs scored on hits—but not runs scored on errors—count when determining an earned run average).

My point is that a lot more mathematical knowledge seems to go into understanding basic baseball statistics than into assessing claims about abortion's share of Planned Parenthood's services, or the number of smoking-related deaths in California. Our math educators don't seem to have let us down when it comes to teaching people the skills needed to understand somewhat complicated baseball statistics, so is it fair to blame them for all the boneheaded numbers that pop up when people talk about social issues? The problem must have some other, more-than-just-mathematical dimension.

This book argues that bad statistics are products of social processes—processes that affect everyone, not just people with whom we disagree. Bad statistics are not simply the result of deficient math skills; very often, they are not caused by someone making incorrect calculations. Senator Kyl did not make a mistake while calculating abortion's share of Planned Parenthood's services, any more than the blogger miscalculated the number of smoking-related deaths in California. Both presented numbers—inviting them to be understood as facts—without giving much thought to what they were saying. Why did this happen?

Understanding how bad numbers get into circulation requires understanding the social arrangements that foster their production and spread—that is, it forces us to think about how statistics are socially constructed.

To better grasp this point, it may help to return to our example of baseball statistics. We cannot talk sensibly about batting averages or earned run averages without understanding the processes by which those figures are produced. To be sure, people need to be able to add, subtract, multiply, and divide to get those numbers. But that's only part of the story. In establishing those figures, baseball fans long ago agreed to count some events (strike-outs, runs caused by hits), even as they exclude others (walks, runs caused by errors); there is a social consensus about how those figures will be calculated. Note, however, that not everyone agrees that the traditional measures are the best way of tracking baseball performance. Some moneyball theorists, for instance, argue that the percentage of time a batter gets on base—a figure that includes walks and being hit by pitches—is a more valuable measure of a batter's worth than the traditional batting average.[9]

In the same way, all statistics are the result not just of mathematical calculations but of social processes that determine what will and won't be counted. When we hear that some government agency has measured the crime rate or the unemployment rate or the poverty rate, we need to realize that that agency has made a series of choices that led to those numbers. We may also hear criticisms that those official statistics aren't really accurate, not because someone has failed to do the calculations correctly, but because the critics think that figures based on different choices would be more valuable. No statistic can be completely understood unless we appreciate the process of social construction that shaped its production.

This means that both the culture warriors and numeracy's advocates understand part—but only part—of the problem. Culture warriors are suspicious of the other guys' numbers, but they tend to assume that their opponents are deliberately distorting the truth. No doubt that happens, but many people seem to be taken in by their own bad statistics. Those who worry about Planned Parenthood's abortion policies or the number of deaths caused by smoking view these as big problems, and it is easy for advocates committed to their causes to tell themselves that "well over 90 percent" and "37 million" are big numbers, so they must be about right. When people who share a concern about abortion or smoking risks talk among themselves, they may forget to think critically about whichever numbers they're using. It is, of course, easy for culture warriors to spot these lapses in the other guys' thinking, but it is also easy for them to overlook or forgive analogous mistakes within their own camp.

Similarly, numeracy advocates are correct when they note that bad statistics flourish because people don't think carefully about numbers, however, these educators are most interested in mistakes in mathematical reasoning. If they ask themselves why these errors occur, their answer is *bias*. But they use the word bias to mean something broader than when culture warriors use the term (as when conservatives denounce liberal bias). For numeracy advocates, any source of inaccuracy—deliberate or inadvertent—constitutes bias. In their view, bad statistics can be products of inadvertent bias (errors in mathematical reasoning that can be reduced through improved mathematics instruction) or deliberate bias (which they tend to view as someone else's problem).

In short, both culture warriors and numeracy advocates define the problem too narrowly. Bad statistics abound, but not just because those other guys are lying weasels or because people lack basic math skills. Bad statistics are produced by people—often sincere, well-meaning people—who aren't thinking critically about what they're saying. Understanding how dubious figures are created and why they thrive requires asking questions about social processes: How do activists mobilize supporters and attract media attention? Under what circumstances do scientific findings gain public notice? How do the media cover social issues? How is the performance of institutions measured and evaluated? And so on. Answering questions of this sort requires going beyond complaining about ideological bias and innumeracy: it forces us to think about the social arrangements—the processes of social construction—that shape all statistics, from the best to the worst.

This book argues that, by focusing attention on the social construction of numbers, sociology can help us understand where flawed figures come from and why they won't go away. This is not to say that sociologists are likely to play the key role in solving the problem. Many quantitatively-inclined sociologists—like many of the researchers who apply statistical reasoning in economics, medicine, psychology, and other disciplines—become fascinated with elaborate, arcane analytic techniques. As I write this, the current issue of the *American Sociological Review,* our discipline's leading journal, contains tables that report the results of complex statistical calculations—"event history analysis and negative binomial regression," "logistic and OLS regression analyses," and so on. For the experts that write these research reports, numbers that purport to describe abortion's share of Planned Parenthood's activities or the number of smoking-related deaths in California are so simpleminded, they hardly qualify as statistics. When sociologists—and their colleagues in other disciplines—teach courses on statistics, their focus tends to be on teaching students how to conduct the most sophisticated analyses, rather than on how to think critically about the simple statistics that shape public understanding of social issues. Everyone may agree that students ought to become critical consumers of numbers, but few want to devote class time to teaching those skills.

Bad statistics about public issues are very common, but they seem to fall between the stools occupied by the various experts we might turn to for help in understanding the problem. Many—not all, but many—culture warriors are part-time critical thinkers: they carefully inspect numbers, but only when those figures seem to challenge their own beliefs. Many—again, not all, but many—numeracy advocates restrict their attention to the role of deficient mathematical reasoning in shaping bad statistics, while dismissing all other sorts of bias as someone else's problem. Similarly, most statistically sophisticated researchers are intent on applying complex analytic techniques to the frontiers of their disciplines; they tend to treat the simple numbers that appear in public debates as beneath their notice. It's not that any of these people like bad statistics—they don't. But no one feels obliged to confront them.

We live in a complicated world, and we need to be able to think critically about its complexity. We can't rely on our narrow personal experiences to tell us what's going on; we need statistics to give us a broader, more accurate view. But if we are going to use numbers, we need to understand the the social processes that produce statistics—and what the limitations of those figures might be. That remains the challenge posed by this book.

NOTES

INTRODUCTION

1. Children's Defense Fund, *The State of America's Children Year-book—1994* (Washington, D.C.: Children's Defense Fund, 1994), p. x.

2. Twain uses the expression in his autobiography, but refers to it as "the remark attributed to Disraeli."

3. Darrell Huff, *How to Lie with Statistics* (New York: Norton, 1954). For a more sophisticated discussion, see A. J. Jaffe and Herbert F. Spirer, *Misused Statistics: Straight Talk for Twisted Numbers* (New York: Dekker, 1987). There are also some outstanding books on specialized topics: on graphs and charts—Edward R. Tufte, *The Visual Display of Quantitative Information* (Cheshire, Conn.: Graphics Press, 1983); on maps—Mark Monmonier, *How to Lie with Maps* (Chicago: University of Chicago Press, 1991); on polls—Herbert Asher, *Polling and the Public: What Every Citizen Should Know,* 3d ed. (Washington, D.C.: Congressional Quarterly Press, 1998). Mark H. Maier's *The Data Game: Controversies in Social Science Statistics,* 3d ed. (Armonk, N.Y.: Sharpe, 1999) explains the most familiar social,

economic, and political measures, and outlines their limitations. There are also various specialized volumes, such as Clive Coleman and Jenny Moynihan, *Understanding Crime Data: Haunted by the Dark Figure* (Buckingham, U.K.: Open University Press, 1996).

4. John Allen Paulos, *Innumeracy: Mathematical Illiteracy and Its Consequences* (New York: Random House, 1988).

CHAPTER 1

1. Timothy J. Gilfoyle, *City of Eros: New York City, Prostitution, and the Commercialization of Sex, 1790–1920* (New York: Norton, 1992), p. 57.

2. Marilynn Wood Hill, *Their Sisters' Keepers: Prostitution in New York City, 1830–1870* (Berkeley and Los Angeles: University of California Press, 1993), p. 27. The various estimates cited are documented in this book and in Gilfoyle, *City of Eros.*

3. Christopher Hewitt, "Estimating the Number of Homeless: Media Misrepresentation of an Urban Problem," *Journal of Urban Affairs* 18 (1996): 432–47.

4. On statistics' history, see: M. J. Cullen, *The Statistical Movement in Early Victorian Britain: The Foundations of Empirical Social Research* (Sussex: Harvester Press, 1975); and Theodore M. Porter, *The Rise of Statistical Thinking, 1820–1900* (Princeton: Princeton University Press, 1986).

5. There are many studies of the social construction of social problems. For introductions to this approach, see: Malcolm Spector and John I. Kitsuse, *Constructing Social Problems* (Menlo Park, Calif.: Cummings, 1977); Joel Best, ed., *Images of Issues: Typifying Contemporary Social Problems,* 2d ed. (Hawthorne, N.Y.: Aldine de Gruyter,

1995); and Donileen R. Loseke, *Thinking about Social Problems* (Hawthorne, N.Y.: Aldine de Gruyter, 1999).

6. On statistics produced by activists and experts, see Neil Gilbert, "Advocacy Research and Social Policy," *Crime and Justice* 20 (1997): 101–48.

7. On powerful institutions' ability to produce statistics that promote their ends, see Cynthia Crossen, *Tainted Truth: The Manipulation of Fact in America* (New York: Simon & Schuster, 1994).

8. Gary Kleck, *Targeting Guns: Firearms and Their Control* (Hawthorne, N.Y.: Aldine de Gruyter, 1997).

9. Paulos, *Innumeracy*, p. 3.

10. John I. Kitsuse and Aaron V. Cicourel, "A Note on the Uses of Official Statistics," *Social Problems* 11 (1963): 131–39; Robert Bogdan and Margret Ksander, "Policy Data as a Social Process," *Human Organization* 39 (1980): 302–9.

11. On suicide recordkeeping, see Jack D. Douglas, *The Social Meanings of Suicide* (Princeton: Princeton University Press, 1967).

12. There are many studies of the effect of organizational practices on statistics produced by the police; for example, see Richard McCleary, Barbara C. Nienstedt, and James M. Erven, "Uniform Crime Reports as Organizational Outcomes," *Social Problems* 29 (1982): 361–72.

CHAPTER 2

1. Albert D. Biderman and Albert J. Riess Jr., "On Exploring the 'Dark Figure' of Crime," *Annals of the American Academy of Political and Social Sciences* 374 (1967): 1–15. Criminologists have used the term "dark figure" for decades; the problem was understood in some

of the earliest criminological writings, e.g., Lambert A. J. Quetelet, *A Treatise on Man and the Development of his Faculties* (Gainesville, Fla.: Scholars' Facsimiles & Reprints, 1969—reproduction of the 1842 English translation of the 1835 French original), p. 82.

2. Quoted in Christopher Jencks, *The Homeless* (Cambridge: Harvard University Press, 1994), p. 2.

3. Examples include claims that there are one million victims of elder abuse each year (Stephen Crystal, "Elder Abuse: The Latest 'Crisis,'" *The Public Interest* 88 [1987]: 56–66), two million missing children (Joel Best, *Threatened Children: Rhetoric and Concern about Child-Victims* [Chicago: University of Chicago Press, 1990]), and, of course, three million homeless persons (Hewitt, "Estimating the Number of Homeless").

4. Scott Adams, *The Dilbert Principle* (New York: Harper Collins, 1996), p. 83.

5. I borrow the expression "number laundering" from David F. Luckenbill.

6. Kathleen S. Lowney and Joel Best, "Stalking Strangers and Lovers: Changing Media Typifications of a New Crime Problem," in *Images of Issues,* 2d ed., ed. Joel Best (Hawthorne, N.Y.: Aldine de Gruyter, 1995), pp. 33–57.

7. Mike Tharp, "In the Mind of a Stalker," *U.S. News & World Report,* February 17, 1992, pp. 28–30.

8. *Sally Jessy Raphael,* "Miss America Stalked," February 15, 1994, Journal Graphics transcript no. 1420.

9. William Sherman, "Stalking," *Cosmopolitan,* April 1994, pp. 198–201.

10. The first serious attempt to measure the national incidence of stalking involved a national survey conducted in late 1995 and early 1996. In this case, the study produced estimates higher than the orig-

inal guesses; the investigators estimated that more than one million women and over 370,000 men experienced stalking annually. Patricia Tjaden and Nancy Thoennes, "Stalking in America: Findings from the National Violence against Women Survey," *National Institute of Justice/Centers for Disease Control and Prevention Research in Brief,* April 1998, p. 3.

11. Hewitt, "Estimating the Number of Homeless."

12. Peter H. Rossi, "No Good Applied Social Research Goes Unpunished," *Society* 25 (November 1987): 73–79.

13. In the 1994 National Crime Victimization Survey, 36 percent of respondents who reported having been raped said they'd reported the crime to the police: Kathleen Maguire and Ann L. Pastore, eds., *Sourcebook of Criminal Justice Statistics, 1996* (Washington, D. C.: Bureau of Justice Statistics, 1997), p. 224. A variety of factors are known to affect reporting: Ronet Bachman, "The Factors Related to Rape Reporting Behavior and Arrest: New Evidence from the National Crime Victimization Survey," *Criminal Justice and Behavior* 25 (1998): 8–29.

14. Mary P. Koss, "The Underdetection of Rape: Methodological Choices Influence Incidence Estimates," *Journal of Social Issues* 48, 1 (1992): 61–76.

15. Max Singer, "The Vitality of Mythical Numbers," *The Public Interest* 23 (1971): 3–9; Peter Reuter, "The Social Costs of the Demand for Quantification," *Journal of Policy Analysis and Management* 5 (1986): 807–12; and Reuter, "The Mismeasurement of Illegal Drug Markets," in *Exploring the Underground Economy,* ed. Susan Pozo (Kalamazoo, Mich.: Upjohn Institute, 1996), pp. 63–80.

16. Some analysts advocate broad definitions precisely because they lead to larger numbers: "most national crime surveys, which define violence in narrow legalistic terms, uncover very low levels of

violence against women. . . . Feminist surveys, on the other hand, that define violence on the basis of women's subjective experiences of violence, including noncriminal and marginally criminal acts, uncover very high levels of violence": Michael D. Smith, "Enhancing the Quality of Survey Data on Violence against Women," *Gender and Society* 8 (1994): pp. 110–11.

17. Joel Best, *Random Violence: How We Talk about New Crimes and New Victims* (Berkeley and Los Angeles: University of California Press, 1999), p. 105.

18. Gordon Hawkins and Franklin E. Zimring, *Pornography in a Free Society* (New York: Cambridge University Press, 1988).

19. On shifting definitions of literacy and illiteracy, see Harvey J. Graff, *The Legacies of Literacy: Continuities and Contradictions in Western Culture and Society* (Bloomington: Indiana University Press, 1987).

20. On competing definitions of homelessness, see: Jencks, *The Homeless*; and James D. Wright, Beth A. Rubin, and Joel A. Devine, *Beside the Golden Door: Policy, Politics, and the Homeless* (Hawthorne, N.Y.: Aldine de Gruyter, 1998).

21. James D. Wright, Peter H. Rossi, and Kathleen Daly, *Under the Gun: Weapons, Crime, and Violence in America* (New York: Aldine, 1983), pp. 215–41; Kleck, *Targeting Guns,* pp. 325–29.

22. Lloyd Stires and Philip J. Klass, "3.7 Million Americans Kidnapped by Aliens?" *Skeptical Inquirer* 17 (Winter 1993): 142–46.

23. Mary Koss, Christine Gidycz, and Nadine Wisniewski, "The Scope of Rape: Incidence and Prevalence of Sexual Aggression and Victimization in a National Sample of Higher Education Students," *Journal of Consulting and Clinical Psychology* 55 (1987): 162–70.

24. Gilbert, "Advocacy Research and Social Policy."

25. Smith, "Enhancing the Quality of Survey Data."

26. Leonard Beeghley, "Illusion and Reality in the Measurement of Poverty," *Social Problems* 31 (1984): 322–33; Patricia Ruggles, *Drawing the Line: Alternative Poverty Measures and Their Implications for Public Policy* (Washington, D.C.: Urban Institute Press, 1990).

27. Michael Fumento refers to this as the *democratization of risk: The Myth of Heterosexual AIDS* (New York: Basic Books, 1990).

CHAPTER 3

1. Carol Lawson, "Doctors Cite Emetic Abuse," *American Anorexia/Bulimia Association Newsletter*, June 1985, p. 1.

2. Christina Hoff Sommers, *Who Stole Feminism?* (New York: Simon & Schuster, 1994), pp. 11–12.

3. U.S. Bureau of the Census, *Statistical Abstract of the United States: 1997*, 117th ed. (Washington, D.C., 1997), p. 96.

4. Michael Kelly, "Playing with Fire," *New Yorker*, July 15, 1996, pp. 28–36.

5. Michael Fumento, "A Church Arson Epidemic? It's Smoke and Mirrors," *Wall Street Journal*, July 9, 1996; James B. Jacobs and Elizabeth E. Joh, "Tremors on the Racial Fault Line: The 1996 Black Church Fires in Retrospect," *Criminal Law Bulletin* 34 (1998): 497–519.

6. James B. Jacobs and Kimberly Potter, *Hate Crimes: Criminal Law and Identity Politics* (New York: Oxford University Press, 1998).

7. Ann Pellegrini, "Rape Is a Bias Crime," *New York Times*, May 27, 1990, p. E-13.

8. Michael J. Berens, "Hatred Is a Crime Many Just Ignore," *Chicago Tribune*, January 11, 1998, pp. 1, 16.

9. Ibid.; Jacobs and Potter, *Hate Crimes*, pp. 55–59.

10. Marty Rimm, "Marketing Pornography on the Information Superhighway," *Georgetown Law Journal* 83 (1995): 1849–1934.

11. Philip Jenkins, *Moral Panic: Changing Concepts of the Child Molester in Modern America* (New Haven: Yale University Press, 1998), pp. 210–11.

12. Dennis Gaboury and Elinor Burkett, "The Secret of St. Mary's," *Rolling Stone,* November 11, 1993, p. 54.

13. Philip Jenkins, *Pedophiles and Priests: Anatomy of a Contemporary Crisis* (New York: Oxford University Press, 1996), p. 80.

14. Marc Riedel, "Counting Stranger Homicides: A Case Study of Statistical Prestidigitation," *Homicide Studies* 2 (1998): 206–19.

15. Philip Jenkins, *Using Murder: The Social Construction of Serial Homicide* (Hawthorne, N.Y.: Aldine de Gruyter, 1994).

16. Riedel, "Counting Stranger Homicides."

17. Joel Best, "The Vanishing White Man: *Workforce 2000* and Tales of Demographic Transformation," in *Tales of the State: Narrative and Contemporary U.S. Politics and Public Policy,* ed. Sanford F. Schram and Philip T. Neisser (Lanham, Md.: Rowman & Littlefield, 1997), pp. 174–83; and William B. Johnstone and Arnold E. Packer, *Workforce 2000: Work and Workers for the Twenty-first Century* (Indianapolis: Hudson Institute, 1987).

18. U.S. Department of Labor, *Workforce 2000: Executive Summary* (Washington, D.C., 1987), p. xiii.

19. Frank Swoboda, "Students of Labor Force Projections Have Been Working without a 'Net,'" *Washington Post,* November 6, 1990, p. A17.

20. Warren Furutani in U.S. House of Representatives, Committee on Education and Labor, *Hearing on H.R. 2235, Workforce 2000 Employment Readiness Act of 1989,* November 3, 1989, p. 69.

21. Lisa M. Schwartz, Steven Woloshin, and H. Gilbert Welch,

"Misunderstandings about the Effects of Race and Sex on Physicians' Referrals for Cardiac Catheterization," *New England Journal of Medicine* 341 (1999): 279–83.

22. The expression "odds ratio" has various meanings in statistics. Sociologists most often use the term when interpreting the results of sophisticated logistic regression analyses. The researchers in this study used the term to refer to a simpler, very different statistic.

23. Alfred C. Kinsey, Wardell B. Pomeroy, and Clyde E. Martin, *Sexual Behavior in the Human Male* (Philadelphia: W. B. Saunders, 1948); Kinsey, Pomeroy, Martin, and Paul H. Gebhard, *Sexual Behavior in the Human Female* (Philadelphia: W. B. Saunders, 1953).

24. Kinsey, Pomeroy, and Martin, *Sexual Behavior in the Human Male,* p. 651.

25. Edward O. Laumann, John H. Gagnon, Robert T. Michael, and Stuart Michaels, *The Social Organization of Sexuality: Sexual Practices in the United States* (Chicago: University of Chicago Press, 1994).

26. For this example, I am indebted to an unpublished paper by Philip Jenkins.

CHAPTER 4

1. Mary Allen and Terri Sanginiti, "Del. Drivers at a Deadly Pace," [Wilmington, Del.] *News Journal,* July 2, 2000, p. A1.

2. Douglas J. Besharov, "Overreporting and Underreporting Are Twin Problems," in *Current Controversies on Family Violence,* ed. Richard J. Gelles and Donileen R. Loseke (Newbury Park, Calif.: Sage, 1993), pp. 257–72; U.S. Bureau of the Census, *Statistical Abstract of the United States: 1997,* 117th ed., p. 219.

3. Ronet Bachman and Linda E. Saltzman, "Violence against Women: Estimates from the Redesigned Survey," *Bureau of Justice Statistics Special Report*, August, 1995.

4. Fred Block and Gene A. Burns, "Productivity as a Social Problem: The Uses and Misuses of Social Indicators," *American Sociological Review* 51 (1986): 767–80.

5. James A. Inciardi, Hilary L. Surratt, and Christine A. Saum, *Cocaine-Exposed Infants* (Thousand Oaks, Calif.: Sage, 1997), pp. 21–38.

6. Fumento, *The Myth of Heterosexual AIDS.*

7. Cheryl L. Maxson and Malcolm W. Klein, "Street Gang Violence: Twice as Great, or Half as Great?" in *Gangs in America,* ed. C. Ronald Huff (Newbury Park, Calif.: Sage, 1990), pp. 71–100.

8. Ray August, "The Mythical Kingdom of Lawyers," *ABA Journal* 78 (September 1992): 72–74.

9. David C. Berliner and Bruce J. Biddle, *The Manufactured Crisis: Myths, Fraud, and the Attack on America's Public Schools* (Reading, Mass.: Addison-Wesley, 1995), pp. 51–63; Gerald W. Bracey, "Are U.S. Students Behind?" *The American Prospect* 37 (March 1998): 64–70.

10. The 2000 census was the first to give respondents the option of indicating they were of mixed racial heritage. On issues of racial classification, see William Petersen, *Ethnicity Counts* (New Brunswick, N.J.: Transaction, 1997).

11. U.S. Bureau of the Census, *Statistical Abstract of the United States, 1997,* 117th ed., p. 201.

12. David M. Heien and David J. Pittman, "The Economic Costs of Alcohol Abuse," *Journal of Studies on Alcohol* 50 (1989): 577.

13. William Fremouw, Ty Callahan, and Jody Kashden, "Adolescent Suicidal Risk," *Suicide and Life Threatening Behavior* 23 (1993): 46.

CHAPTER 5

1. Best, *Threatened Children,* pp. 45–64.

2. Scott Bowles, "Park Police Can Count on a Disputed Crowd Figure," *Washington Post,* October 15, 1995, p. B1.

3. Stephen A. Holmes, "After March, Lawmakers Seek Commission on Race Relations," *Washington Post,* October 18, 1995, p. A1.

4. Christopher B. Daly and Hamil R. Harris, "Boston U. Sets March at 837,000," *Washington Post,* October 28, 1995, p. C3.

5. Herbert A. Jacobs, "To Count a Crowd," *Columbia Journalism Review* 6 (Spring 1967): 37–40.

6. Leef Smith and Wendy Melillo, "If It's Crowd Size You Want, Park Service Says Count It Out," *Washington Post,* October 13, 1996, p. A34. In 1997, sociologists Clark McPhail and John McCarthy estimated that the crowd size for a Promise Keepers' rally—according to McPhail "much larger than the Million Man March crowd"—was 480,000; one minister in the crowd insisted there were 2.5 million present. Linda Wheeler, "Unofficial Estimates Point to Crowded Day on the Mall," *Washington Post,* October 5, 1997, p. A17.

7. For introductions to contemporary census issues, see: Margo J. Anderson and Stephen E. Fienberg, *Who Counts? The Politics of Census-Taking in Contemporary America* (New York: Russell Sage Foundation, 1999); Harvey Choldin, *Looking for the Last Percent: The Controversy over Census Undercounts* (New Brunswick, N.J.: Rutgers University Press, 1994); and Peter Skerry, *Counting on the Census? Race, Group Identity, and the Evasion of Politics* (Washington, D.C.: Brookings Institution Press, 2000).

8. For introductions to contemporary income distribution issues, see: Peter Gottschalk, "Inequality, Income Growth, and Mobility: The Basic Facts," *Journal of Economic Perspectives* 11 (Spring 1997): 21–40; Maier, *The Data Game,* pp. 144–65; Martina

Morris and Bruce Western, "Inequality in Earnings at the Close of the Twentieth Century," *Annual Review of Sociology* 25 (1999): 623–57; and Stephen J. Rose, *Social Stratification in the United States,* rev. ed. (New York: New Press, 2000).

9. For example, contrast the interpretations of statistics related to race in Stephan Thernstrom and Abigail Thernstrom, *America in Black and White* (New York: Simon & Schuster, 1997), and Stephen R. Shalom, "Dubious Data: The Thernstroms on Race in America," *Race and Society* 1 (1998): 125–57.

10. William J. Bennett, *The Index of Leading Cultural Indicators: American Society at the End of the Twentieth Century,* rev. ed. (New York: Broadway Books, 1999); Marc Miringoff and Marque-Luisa Miringoff, *The Social Health of the Nation: How America Is Really Doing* (New York: Oxford University Press, 1999). Examples of other specialized volumes include: Women's Action Coalition, *WAC Stats: The Facts about Women* (New York: New Press, 1993); Joni Seager, *The State of Women in the World Atlas,* 2d ed. (London: Penguin, 1997); Farai Chideya, *Don't Believe the Hype: Fighting Cultural Misinformation about African-Americans* (New York: Plume, 1995); Doug Henwood, *The State of the U.S.A. Atlas* (New York: Simon & Schuster, 1994); and Bennett L. Singer and David Deschamps, *Gay & Lesbian Stats: A Pocket Guide of Facts and Figures* (New York: New Press, 1994).

11. Bennett, *Index of Leading Cultural Indicators,* p. 4.

12. Miringoff and Miringoff, *Social Health of the Nation,* p. 5.

13. Miringoff and Miringoff compare economic and social indicators: *Social Health of the Nation,* pp. 11–14. Obviously, all economic statistics must confront the standard statistical issues—definition, measurement, sampling, and so on. For an overview of the limitations of many economic statistics, see Maier, *The Data Game.*

14. Miringoff and Miringoff, *Social Health of the Nation,* pp. 84–85.

15. Bennett, *Index of Leading Cultural Indicators,* p. 74.

16. Women's Action Coalition, *WAC Stats,* pp. 21, 25.

17. On occasion, the press does investigative stories that call dubious statistics into question. Examples include the *Denver Post's* 1985 stories on activists' exaggerated estimates of the numbers of missing children, and the *Philadelphia Inquirer's* 1999 exposés of systematic underreporting of crime rates by the Philadelphia police.

AFTERWORD

1. A summary of this incident, including a video clip of Kyl's speech, a summary of statistics reported by Planned Parenthood, and a link to coverage of the explanation offered by the senator's office, may be found at PolitiFact.com. "Jon Kyl Says Abortion Services Are 'Well Over 90 Percent of What Planned Parenthood Does,'" last modified April 8, 2011, accessed March 11, 2012, http://www.politifact.com/truth-o-meter/statements/2011/apr/08/jon-kyl/jon-kyl-says-abortion-services-are-well-over-90-pe/.

2. "Services," Planned Parenthood Federation of America, accessed March 11, 2012, http://www.plannedparenthood.org/files/PPFA/PP_Services.pdf.

3. Rachel K. Jones and Kathryn Kooistra, "Abortion Incidence and Access to Services in the United States, 2008," *Perspectives on Sexual and Reproductive Health* 43 (2011): 41–50.

4. Recent examples include: Laura Amico, "Understanding MPD's 94% Homicide Closure Rate," Homicide Watch D.C., last modified December 30, 2011, accessed March 11, 2012, http://homicide

watch.org/2011/12/30/understanding-mpds-94-homicide-closure-rate/; Greg Toppo, Denise Amos, Jack Gillum and Jodi Upton, "When Scores Seem Too Good to Be True: To Help Students and Schools Make the Grade, Are Some Educators Crossing the Line?," *USA Today,* March 7, 2011; and Kevin Selig, "Greed, Negligence, or System Failure: Credit Rating Agencies and the Financial Crisis," Kenan Institute for Ethics, last modified 2011, accessed March 11, 2012, http://www.duke.edu/web/kenanethics/CaseStudies/Moodys.pdf.

5. Recent examples of such critiques include: Michael Blastland and Andrew Dilnot, *The Numbers Game: The Commonsense Guide to Understanding Numbers in the News, in Politics, and in Life* (New York: Gotham, 2009); Bernard L. Madison and Lynn Arthur Steen, eds., *Calculation and Context: Quantitative Literacy and Its Implications for Teacher Education* (Washington D.C.: Mathematical Association of America, 2008); and Steven Woloshin, Lisa M. Schwartz, and H. Gilbert Welch, *Know Your Chances: Understanding Health Statistics* (Berkeley: University of California Press, 2008).

6. Kimberly Chin, "States with Smoker-Friendly Laws," Main Street, last modified May 5, 2011, accessed March 11, 2012, http://www.mainstreet.com/slideshow/family/family-health/states-smoker-friendly-laws-0.

7. See, for instance: Jason Linkins, "Jon Kyl Is Sorry If He Gave Anyone The Impression That The Things He Says In Public Are Factual," *Huffington Post,* last modified June 8, 2011, accessed March 11, 2012, http://www.huffingtonpost.com/2011/04/08/jon-kyl-is-sorry-if-he-ga_n_846941.html; Steve Ertelt, "Politifact Misleads in Bashing Jon Kyl Over Planned Parenthood," LifeNews.com, last modified April 11, 2011, accessed March 11, 2012, http://www.lifenews.com/2011/04/11/politifact-misleads-in-bashing-jon-kyl-over-planned-parenthood/.

8. Paulos, *Innumeracy;* Madison and Steen, *Calculation and Context.*

9. Michael Lewis, *Moneyball: The Art of Winning an Unfair Game* (New York: Norton, 2003).

INDEX

Compositor:	BookMatters, Berkeley
Text:	9/15.25 Utopia
Display:	ITC Officina Sans Book
Printer and binder:	Maple-Vail Book Manufacturing Company